THE CHILDREN OF IZIEU:
A Human Tragedy

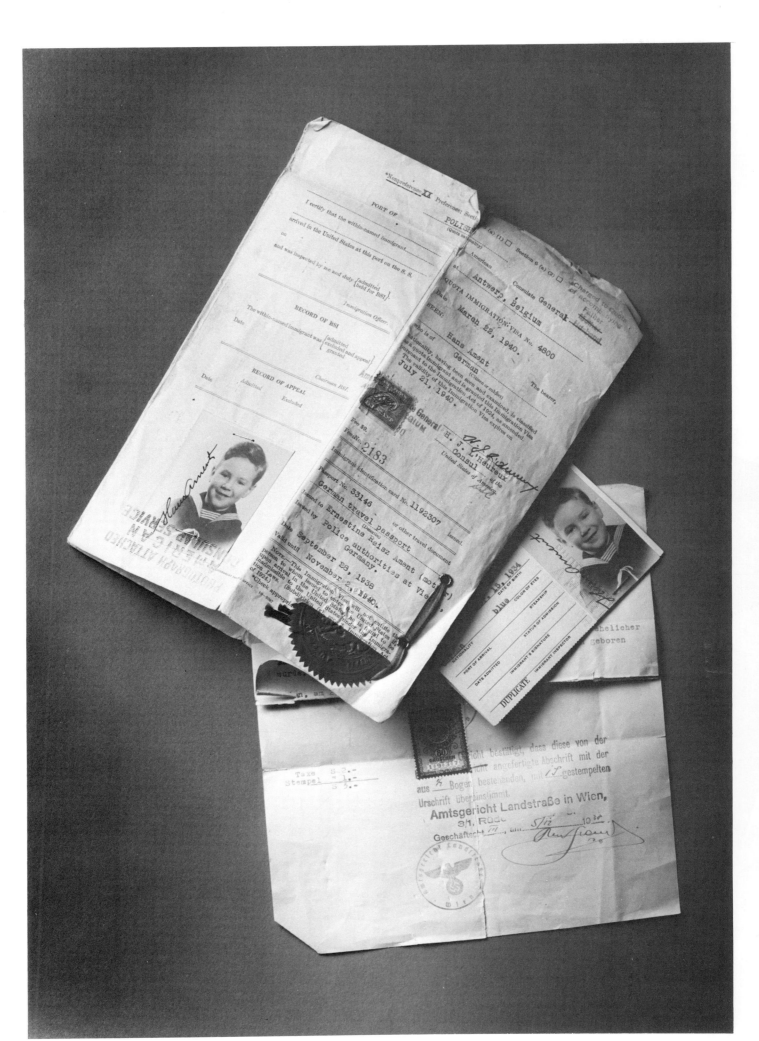

THE CHILDREN OF IZIEU: A Human Tragedy

Serge Klarsfeld

Foreword by Beate and Serge Klarsfeld

Translated by Kenneth Jacobson

Harry N. Abrams, Inc., Publishers, New York

Editor: Beverly Fazio
Designer: Samuel N. Antupit

Library of Congress Cataloging in Publication Data

Klarsfeld, Serge, 1935–
   The children of Izieu.

   Translation of: Les enfants d'Izieu.
   1. Jews—France—Izieu—Persecutions.   2. Holocaust,
Jewish (1939–1945)—France—Izieu.   3. Jewish children
—France—Izieu.   4. World War, 1939–1945—Deportations
from France.   5. Barbie, Klaus, 1913–
6. War criminals—Germany—Biography.   7. Izieu
(France)—Ethnic relations. I. Title.
DS135.F85195513 1985   940.53′15′03924   85-7366
ISBN 0-8109-2307-6

Photograph credits: The group photographs at Izieu were supplied by Paulette Paillarès, Paul Niederman, and Henry Alexander. The individual photographs that were taken elsewhere
were supplied by members of the victims' families. The recent
photographs of the house at Izieu were taken by Emmanuel
Lulin.

On the cover: Many of the forty-four children and six counselors who were arrested, deported, and murdered in 1944
can be seen in this group portrait taken at Izieu during a
celebration in the summer of 1943.

On page 2: The United States entry visa of Hans Ament, age
ten. The German invasion of Belgium cut off his family's
escape to America, and they were forced to flee instead to
France, where Hans later found his way to Izieu.

The chapter "Two Mothers of Izieu Struggle to Bring Barbie
to Justice" is reprinted from *Wherever They May Be!* by Beate
Klarsfeld, translated from the French by Monroe Stearns and
Natalie Gerardi, by permission of the publisher, Vanguard
Press, Inc. Copyright © 1975 by Beate Klarsfeld.

The chapter "Barbie Unpunished" previously appeared as
Serge Klarsfeld's Afterword to *Klaus Barbie* by Tom Bower,
published in France by Calmann-Levy. Used by permission.

	Name		Age	Birthplace	Convoy Number
The 44 children of Izieu arrested April 6, 1944; all of them were Jews, and all were deported and murdered	ADELSHEIMER	Sami	5	Germany	71
	AMENT	Hans	10	Austria	75
	ARONOWICZ	Nina	11	Belgium	71
	BALSAM	Jean-Paul	10	France	71
	BALSAM	Max-Marcel	12	France	71
	BENASSAYAG	Elie	10	Algeria	71
	BENASSAYAG	Esther	12	Algeria	71
	BENASSAYAG	Jacob	8	Algeria	71
	BENGUIGUI	Jacques	12	Algeria	71
	BENGUIGUI	Jean-Claude	5	Algeria	71
	BENGUIGUI	Richard	7	Algeria	71
	BENTITOU	Barouk-Raoul	12	Algeria	71
	BULKA	Albert	4	Belgium	71
	BULKA	Majer	13	Poland	71
	FRIEDLER	Lucienne	5	Belgium	76
	GAMIEL	Egon	9	Germany	71
	GERENSTEIN	Liliane	11	France	71
	GERENSTEIN	Maurice	13	France	71
	GOLDBERG	Henri-Chaïm	13	France	71
	GOLDBERG	Joseph	12	France	71
	HALAUNBRENNER	Claudine	5	France	76
	HALAUNBRENNER	Mina	8	France	76
	HALPERN	Georges	8	Austria	71
	HIRSCH	Arnold	17	Germany	73
	KARGEMAN	Isidore	10	France	71
	KROCHMAL	Liane	6	Austria	71
	KROCHMAL	Renate	8	Austria	71
	LEINER	Max	8	Austria	71
	LEVAN-REIFMAN	Claude	10	France	71
	LÖBMANN	Fritz	15	Germany	71
	LUZGART	Alice-Jacqueline	10	France	75
	MERMELSTEIN	Marcel	7	Belgium	74
	MERMELSTEIN	Paula	10	Belgium	74
	REIS	Theodor	16	Germany	73
	SADOWSKI	Gilles	8	France	71
	SPIEGEL	Martha	10	Austria	71
	SPIEGEL	Senta	9	Austria	71
	SPRINGER	Sigmund	8	Austria	71
	SZULKLAPER	Sarah	11	France	71
	TETELBAUM	Herman	10	Belgium	71
	TETELBAUM	Max	12	Belgium	71
	WELTNER	Charles	9	France	75
	WERTHEIMER	Otto	12	Germany	71
	ZUCKERBERG	Emile	5	Belgium	71
The adults from Izieu who were deported and murdered	FEIGER	Lucie	49	France	72
	FRIEDLER	Mina	32	Poland	76
	LEVAN-REIFMAN	Sarah	36	Rumania	71
	REIFMAN	Eva	61	Rumania	71
	REIFMAN	Moïse	63	Rumania	71
	ZLATIN	Miron	39	Russia	73
Izieu's sole survivor of deportation	FELDBLUM	Laja	26	Poland	71
The escapee from the Izieu raid	REIFMAN	Léon	30	Rumania	

CONTENTS

FOREWORD

In the cases we have undertaken, our goal has always been twofold: to institute legal proceedings, and to contribute to history by assembling and publishing an accurate documentary record. Of this dual quest the present volume was born. For this book, dedicated to the memory of the children of Izieu, is the fruit of long and patient research. And it was for the children of Izieu —and for them alone—that we tracked down and unmasked Klaus Barbie, and played a part in bringing about his forced return to Lyon.

From the time we located Barbie, in 1971, we have been in a position to bring to light the different stages of his SS career, to establish that he enjoyed the protection of the American Special Services while in Germany after the war, and to determine the circumstances in which he left Europe to settle in South America.

In anticipation of Barbie's arrival in France, we made a systematic search for the original of the telex he sent to the anti-Jewish section of the Gestapo in Paris, reporting that the home for Jewish children at Izieu had been liquidated. And, in the end, we found it.

Assisted by our colleague Charles Libman and by Richard Zelmati, our affiliate in Lyon, we have brought to the prosecution of this case all the legal and evidentiary assistance which might reasonably have been expected of us as attorneys for the numerous associate plaintiffs:* the families of the children of Izieu.

With the same persistence, we tried to find out who each of those children was. We did not content ourselves with the information on the commemorative plaque which was mounted on the house at Izieu after the war, and which lists forty-nine victims of the raid perpetrated by the Lyon Gestapo; instead, we undertook to locate members of each of these children's families in order to establish accurate vital statistics, to learn how and why they found their way to Izieu, and, if possible, to become acquainted with their faces and personalities. Only when we had succeeded down to the last case did we call an end to our investigations.

*In French law, an associate plaintiff (partie civile) is a relative of an aggrieved party who has pressed charges against the person or persons he or she holds responsible for the injury, and who may participate actively in the state's prosecution stemming from the original complaint.

This research has permitted us to rectify a number of errors that appear on the commemorative plaque. Over three-quarters of the ages and several of the first names it lists are incorrect. Furthermore, one child who was arrested, Fritz Löbmann, does not appear at all; he seems to have been forgotten. For Barbie's telex of April 6, 1944, speaks of fifty-one arrests—and we have established that there were, in fact, forty-four children and seven adults taken.

In gathering the information upon which these corrections are based, as well as photographs of the children and letters they had written, we were led on a worldwide search. Those acting as parties to the case on behalf of the children of Izieu live not only in France, but in the United States, Israel, Australia, and Brazil.

We have taken this action lest anyone claim—as some have already dared to do—that these children never existed at all, or that they were neither arrested, deported, nor murdered; lest anyone assert that these deported children were not Jewish, or that there were non-Jewish children deported among them; and lest anyone hold to the text of the commemorative plaque, which omits the reason for their arrest and martyrdom: the fact that they were Jews. This, no one could guess upon reading the plaque's epigram: "Let the defense and the love of my fatherland be my defense before Thee, O Lord." Such an oath could be sworn by all who fight for a national cause, and who believe in God. But it does not apply to the children of Izieu, twenty-three of whom were stateless, and only twenty-one French: they took no part in efforts to defend a fatherland that in the majority of cases was not their own.

Forty-four children deported—no mere statistic, but rather forty-four tragedies which continue to cause us pain some forty years after the event. For having, with malice aforethought, put an untimely end to the lives of these children, Klaus Barbie has been hunted down and arrested, and for this he shall be judged.

Beate and Serge Klarsfeld

We extend our gratitude to Dr. Cynthia Haft of Yad Vashem in Jerusalem for her most effective help in locating the families of the children of Izieu.

Left and opposite: The monument to the children of Izieu. Below: The commemorative plaque mounted in April 1946 on the house at Izieu. The text reads as follows:

On April 6, 1944, Maundy Thursday, 43 children from the house at Izieu were arrested by the Germans, with their guardians, then deported on April 15, 1944. Forty-one children and five of their guardians were exterminated in the gas chambers at Ausschwitz [sic]. The director of the home and two boys were executed in the fortress at Revel [a misspelling of Reval, the French name for Tallin, Estonia].

Let the defense and the love of my fatherland be my defense before Thee, O Lord.

LE 6 AVRIL 1944, JOUR DU JEUDI-SAINT 43 ENFANTS DE LA MAISON D'IZIEU ETAIENT ARRETES PAR LES ALLEMANDS, AVEC LEURS MAITRES, PUIS DEPORTES LE 15 AVRIL 1944. QUARANTE ET UN ENFANTS ET CINQ DE LEURS MAITRES FURENT EXTERMINES DANS LES CHAMBRES A GAZ D'AUSSCHWITZ. LE DIRECTEUR DE LA COLONIE ET DEUX GARÇONS FURENT FUSILLES DANS LA FORTERESSE DE REVEL.

REIFMANN-LEVAN CLAUDE 11Ans	BEN TITOU RAOUL 13Ans	BEN ASSAYAG ESTHER 13Ans
TEITELBAUM MAX 13	BULKA MARCEL 14	HALAUBRENNER CLAUDINE 5
TEITELBAUM ARMAND 11	BULKA ALBERT 5	HALAUBRENNER NINA 9
AMENT JEAN 11	HALPERM GEORGES 9	LUZGARD JACQUELINE 12
ZUCKERBERG EMILE 6	MERMELSTEIN MARCEL 8	MERMELSTEIN PAULETTE 12
SPRINGER ZYGMUND 8	GERENSTEIN MAURICE 14	SZULZKLAPPER SUZANNE 12
ADELSHEIMER SAMUEL 7	GOLDBERG HENRI 14	SPIEGEL MARTHE 11
GAMIEL EDMOND 11	GOLDBERG JOSEPH 12	SPIEGEL SANTA 9
SADOVSKI GILLES 9	BALSAM MAX 13	GERENSTEIN LILIANE 11
LEINER MAX 9	BALSAM JEAN 11	
KARGEMAN ISIDORE 11	WELTNER CHARLES 10	
VERTHEIMER OTTO 13	HIRSCH ARNOLD 18	REIFMANN MOÏSE 64
BEN ASSAYAG ELIE 11	REISS THEO 17	REIFMANN NOVA 60
BEN ASSAYAG JACOB 10	FRIEDLER LUCIENNE 5	REIFMANN SUZANNE 38
BEN CUICUI JACQUES 13	KROCHMAL RENATHE 9	FEIGER LUCIE 50
BEN CUICUI JEAN-CLAUDE 6	KROCHMAL LIANE 7	FRIEDLER MARIE 36
BEN CUICUI RICHARD 8	APONOWICZ MINA 12	ZLATIN MIRON 40

QUE LA DEFENSE ET L'AMOUR DE MA PATRIE SOIENT MA DEFENSE DEVANT TOI SEIGNEUR

Two years following the arrest of these ill-fated children and their deportation to Auschwitz—where all were killed—a monument was erected in their memory not far from the village of Izieu, in the department of Ain.

The following is an excerpt from a description of the monument which appeared in the local press in 1946:

The monument erected in memory of the children of Izieu stands within the municipal limits of Bregnier-Cordon, at the head of the road to Lelinaz. Of local stone, it is very simple and sober of line, in keeping with the wishes of Mrs. Zlatin and the members of the Committee. Its triangular column, nearly five meters high, carries an inscription on each of its faces [sic]:

> *To the memory of the forty-three children of the home at Izieu, of their director, and of their five guardians, arrested by the Germans April 6, 1944, and exterminated in the camps or executed in German prisons.*

* * *

> *Wayfarer, gather up thy thoughts!*
> *And forget not the martyrdom of these innocents,*
> *That the place where they once lived*
> *Remain sacred to thee for all time.*

* * *

> *Every man is a piece of the continent,*
> *A part of the main;*
> *Any man's death diminishes me,*
> *Because I am involved in mankind.*

Desecration in Ain
The Children of Izieu
(From our regional correspondent)

Lyon—Three weeks after the desecration of a monument erected in Ain in memory of fifty victims of Nazism—forty-three of them children—an inquiry by the detective bureau of the gendarmery at Belley has not turned up the slightest hint of an answer to the question which the populace is asking itself: Who has dared?

Who is so filled with hate as to defile, in effect, the memory of these forty-three youngsters aged from five to twelve years, almost all of them Jews, arrested April 6, 1944—Holy Thursday—by a detail under the command of Klaus Barbie? Who has daubed the enormous swastikas on the modest granite pillar, erected at the crossroads where Bregnier-Cordon meets Izieu? Who has attempted, in a sense, to do to death a second time these little victims, who, in the trucks which carried them toward the crematory ovens of Auschwitz, sang "You'll Never Take Alsace-Lorraine"?

From the Paris daily *Le Monde*, 1979

THE "FINAL SOLUTION" IN FRANCE

When France surrendered to Germany in June 1940, the majority of its territory was divided into two jurisdictions: an Occupied Zone under the direct authority of the Germans, and an Unoccupied, or Free Zone officially under French rule. Excepted were Alsace and a large part of Lorraine, annexed outright by Germany, and two departments in the extreme northwest of the country, assigned to the Brussels-based German Military Command for Belgium and Northern France.

France's Occupied Zone, which included much of the north of the country and its Atlantic seaboard, was administered by the German Military Commander for France, located in Paris. Also in Paris were the German Embassy, whose function was to advise the military command on political matters, and the headquarters of the German security and intelligence apparatus, known as the Sipo-SD (Sicherheitspolizei und Sicherheitsdienst, or Security Police and Security Service). The Sipo-SD, presided over by the B.d.S. (Befehlshaber der Sipo-SD—Commander of the Sipo-SD), came under the RSHA (Reichssicherheitshauptamt, the Reich Main Security Office) in Berlin. The RSHA was in turn a division of the SS (Schutzstaffel—Protection Staff), the "Black Shirts" or elite guard of the Nazi party. The Gestapo (Geheime Staatspolizei, or Secret State Police), a branch of the Sipo-SD, was number IV of seven bureaus of the RSHA.

The Free Zone, which covered most of central and southern France, was under the jurisdiction of the French government, headquartered in Vichy. All French territory was subject to Vichy's laws, as long as those laws remained consistent with German regulations in the Occupied Zone.

A leading military figure of World War I, Marshal Philippe Pétain, became "chief" of this new "French State" in June 1940. Vichy's first head of government was Pierre Laval; replaced in 1940 by Admiral François Darlan, Laval returned to office in April 1942, staying on until he fled to Germany in August 1944.

From the beginning, and without pressure from the Germans, the Vichy régime enacted a series of measures that made its hostility to Jews—particularly those of foreign birth—abundantly clear: as early as July 1940, the naturalization of foreign-born Jews could be revoked; from August of the same year, anti-Semitic propaganda was given free rein; a law of October 3, 1940, defined "Jew" on the basis of racial criteria and excluded Jews from many public service jobs and professions; and a law of October 4, 1940, allowed French police to arbitrarily arrest "any foreigner of the Jewish race."

Vichy reacted to German pressure as well. From September 1940 to August 1942, the Gestapo's Office for Jewish Affairs in France—Department IV J, later IV B—was headed by Theodor Dannecker, who maintained direct contact with his boss, Adolf Eichmann, the head of the Gestapo's anti-Jewish section at the RSHA in Berlin. Through Helmut Knochen, the head of B.d.S. in Paris, and Kurt Lischka, Knochen's deputy, Dannecker put both direct and indirect pressure on the French government, providing the impetus behind "The Final Solution to the Jewish Question" in France.

It was at Dannecker's urging that French officials took a census of Jews in the Occupied Zone at the end of 1940; Jews living in the Free Zone were counted after the promulgation of a law broadening the definition of "Jew" the following year. And again under pressure from the Germans, the Vichy government set up the CGQJ (Commissariat-Général aux Questions Juives, or Commissariat-General for Jewish Affairs), which was, in effect, a ministry of Jewish affairs. It also established an anti-Jewish police force and an umbrella organization grouping Jewish institutions, the UGIF (Union Générale des Israélites de France, or General Union of French Jews), which was accountable to the French state.

Mass arrests of Jews were inaugurated in May 1941 in the Paris area: 3,733 men, hailing from Austria, Czechoslovakia, and above all, Poland, were sent to Pithiviers and Beaune-la-Rolande, two camps near Orléans in the Occupied Zone that were, however, under French administration. A major roundup took place in the streets of Paris on August 20 of the same year; this time, 4,078 men, including more than 1,000 of French nationality, were placed in Drancy, a camp in a suburb of Paris, which was administered by the French until July 1943. On December 12, 1941, another 700 French Jews were arrested and sent to the camp at Compiègne, where, as at Drancy, inmates were subjected to abominable living conditions.

The first deportations of Jews from France—allegedly in retaliation for terrorist attacks—took place on March 27, 1942, when 1,112 were transported by train to Auschwitz. Four more convoys, of around one thousand each, were to leave France for Auschwitz that June.

In the meantime, the German police apparatus in France had been reinforced with the addition of Kurt Albrecht Oberg, who, as Higher SS and Police Leader, outranked Knochen, and another SS officer, Herbert Hagen. At a meeting held June 11, 1942, in Berlin, plans were made calling for wide-scale arrests and the deportation of one hundred thousand Jews from France—a figure reduced to forty thousand the next week for lack of trains. In this first major phase of the Final Solution in France, Dannecker intended to include both French and non-French Jews, aged mainly between sixteen and forty-five; but he had already begun laying plans for the later deportation of children.

However, in early June, the French population of the Occupied Zone had vigorously protested the German decree requiring most Jews—French and foreign alike—to wear the yellow star, and Vichy subsequently declined to pass a similar ordinance. Then the French government refused to arrest French Jews in the Free Zone and seemed unwilling to let French police make such arrests in the Occupied Zone. Dannecker became furious. Eichmann came to Paris for consultation, arriving on June 30, 1942; the following day, however, plans to deport French Jews were scuttled by Knochen. Knochen was concerned with keeping the peace in order to guarantee France's economic collaboration in the German war effort; a realist, he feared that Vichy might actually prevent its police force from cooperating in the Occupied Zone, thus creating a serious rift. At the same time, he was well aware that the relatively small German police force was not equipped to make the arrests on its own.

Knochen's desire to stay in the shadow of the French police coincided with that of Vichy's new top police official, René Bousquet, to reach an agreement with the Germans that would extend his control of the French police into the Occupied Zone. Bousquet knew that a clash with the Germans, one potential result of the failure of a roundup carried out unaided by the French police, could prevent the accord he wanted. He therefore concluded an agreement with Knochen under which French police would arrest 22,000 stateless Jews living in Paris; French Jews were to be exempt. Bousquet also promised to round up and deliver to the Germans all stateless Jews living in the Free Zone. As Jews from Central and Eastern Europe were either being stripped of their citizenships by their countries of origin or denaturalized by Vichy, huge numbers were to be affected.

Laval, whose instructions Bousquet had already exceeded, reaffirmed the Bousquet-Knochen agreement on July 4, and offered to hand over to the Germans the children of stateless Jews living in the Free Zone; in addition, he claimed not to be concerned with the future of children of stateless Jews living in the Occupied Zone. Thus, Vichy's head of government gave the Nazis a free hand to deport thousands of children of French nationality as well.

Despite detailed preparations by a Franco-German team, a roundup on July 16 and 17, 1942, in Paris failed to fill Bousquet's quota of 22,000. Still, 13,152 Jews—including 4,115 children—were arrested in this roundup, known by the name of the bicycling stadium where many of them were temporarily imprisoned, the Vélodrome d'Hiver. On the second day, representatives of the French police, led by Bousquet's delegate in the Occupied Zone, Jean Leguay, insisted that the children be deported with their parents—or, if their parents were deported beforehand, that they be deported alone. This measure was aimed at assuring that the convoys, now leaving for Auschwitz three times per week, would be full; it would spare the French police the trouble of either lodging the children or arresting additional Jewish adults to be deported in their stead.

Three days later, on July 20, Eichmann agreed to take the children within a few weeks. At the end of July, French police bludgeoned Jewish mothers at Beaune-la-Rolande and Pithiviers into giving up their children. The mothers were deported first; the children were then brought to Drancy in a pitiful state and mixed into convoys with adults so that it would appear that families were being deported together.

The thousands of foreign-born Jews who had been confined since 1940 in such squalid prison camps as Gurs, Rivesaltes, and

Number of Deportees from France by Age

Age of deportees (Names from lists)	Number of deportees				
	Convoys of 1942	Convoys of 1943	Convoys of 1944	Total	%
Under 6 years	1,102	393	398	1,893	2.7%
6–12 years	2,807	527	795	4,129	5.8%
13–17 years	2,514	757	854	4,125	5.8%
18–29 years	4,607	2,521	1,851	8,979	12.7%
30–44 years	14,883	4,585	3,618	23,086	32.6%
45–59 years	11,599	4,661	3,711	19,971	28.2%
60–80 years	2,255	3,354	2,851	8,460	11.9%
Over 80 years	58	47	122	227	0.3%
TOTAL for whom ages are known	39,825	16,845	14,200	70,870	100.0%
Ages unknown	2,530	196	1,065	3,791	
Names not appearing on lists (minimum estimate)	300		760	1,060	
TOTAL NUMBER OF DEPORTEES				75,721	

Les Milles in the Free Zone now began to face deportation. Some of these internees—three thousand of whose number had died of cold and malnutrition over the two previous winters—were joined with victims of a major sweep through the Free Zone held August 26, 1942, to make up the total of ten thousand stateless Jews whom Vichy handed over shortly thereafter.

Next, the occupation authorities obtained permission from the German foreign ministry in Berlin to arrest Jews from the Baltic countries; after that, Jews from Belgium, Holland, Rumania, and Greece were seized during sudden raids conducted by the Paris police. In addition, thousands of French Jews were deported after having been found in violation of one of the many strict laws that ruled out for all Jews—not only the foreign born—the possibility of leading a normal life in society. The Germans' overriding desire was simply to fill the trains.

In fact, following a meeting at Gestapo headquarters in Berlin on August 28, the Germans planned to deport one convoy per day, starting September 15. But the French people, traditionally committed to humanitarian values, had been scandalized at seeing their own police, their own soldiers, even their firemen hunt down Jews in the Free Zone. Important clergymen, notably Monsignor Jules-Gérard Saliège, archbishop of Toulouse, and Monsignor Pierre-Marie Théas, bishop of Montauban, protested vigorously against the violation of human rights. Cardinal Pierre-Marie Gerlier, archbishop of Lyon, protected Jewish children; many Jewish mothers entrusted their children to Christian militants, who, waiting at the train station in Lyon, convinced them that their final destination was certain death.

At the beginning of September 1942, faced with an increasingly indignant French public, Laval and Pétain balked at the German plan. In order to keep to the October schedule, arrests of French Jews would have had to be stepped up; fearing for the future of his régime, Laval refused. With Knochen absent, Heinz Röthke, Dannecker's supposedly less-fanatical successor at the Office for Jewish Affairs in Paris, tried to lay the groundwork for a massive roundup of French Jews planned for September 22. But Knochen convinced Heinrich Himmler, head of the SS, to avoid pushing Laval toward extreme concessions and

thus forcing his hand. As a result, French Jews were not to be arrested, and Laval would no longer be obliged to meet quotas, as he had been in late June.

Nonetheless, by the end of the year, more than 42,000 Jews—6,000 of them children—had been deported from France. The sheer volume of the deportations—33,000 within a period of eleven weeks, from July 15 to September 30, 1942—makes clear the cooperation of the French government and its police in the German endeavor. In addition, the total lack of German retaliation for Laval's refusal to accede to the proposed September roundup suggests that in July—only two months earlier—the head of the French government might successfully have resisted German demands.

In November 1942, the Germans moved across the Line of Demarcation to take over the formerly unoccupied Free Zone; from then on, the Occupied and Free Zones were known as the North and South. Italian troops occupied the Savoy and French Riviera regions; there they stayed, protecting the Jews under their authority, until Italy surrendered in September 1943 and the Germans moved in.

In 1943, seventeen thousand Jews were deported from France; fifteen thousand more were deported the next year, following sporadic sweeps by the French police force, which was becoming ever more reluctant as an Allied victory seemed increasingly assured. The Milice, a paramilitary organization used against the Resistance and the Jews, along with a special commando group dispatched by Eichmann and led by a veteran of the Final Solution in Austria and Salonika, Alois Brunner, helped carry out mass arrests and deportations during this period. Despite such efforts, however, the campaign to extirpate the Jews proved less effective in France than in the East, due in part to growing opposition from the French population in 1943 and 1944.

In all, the Germans deported over 75,000 Jews from France, shipping most of them to Auschwitz in boxcars, in convoys close to a thousand strong. Including those who perished without leaving its borders, 80,000 of the 320,000 Jews living in France in 1940 died as a result of the Final Solution.

THEY WERE ALL JEWS

Two mothers of children from Izieu, Mrs. Ita-Rosa Halaunbrenner and Mrs. Fortunée Benguigui (right foreground, left to right), were present at Izieu on April 8, 1984, for the ceremony marking the fortieth anniversary of the raid. In the black overcoat (center) is Théo Klein, president of the CRIF, which organized the commemoration; Klein was active in efforts to save Jewish children during the war. To Klein's right is CRIF director Jacqueline Keller. The speaker is Serge Klarsfeld, a member of the executive committee of the CRIF.

Excerpts from a speech delivered by Serge Klarsfeld at Izieu on April 8, 1984, during a ceremony organized by C.R.IF (Conseil Representatif des Institutions Juives de France, or Representative Council of Jewish Institutions of France), a body that represents the political interests of France's Jewish community.

Here, forty years ago—on April 6, 1944—an episode took place in the all-out war waged by the Nazis against the Jewish people, a war referred to as 'The Final Solution to the Jewish Question."

Forty-four children and seven adults were arrested by the Lyon Gestapo, which sent them straightaway to Drancy for deportation to the extermination camps, thereby sealing their sentence of death. There was one lone survivor. Léa Feldblum, a counselor, told me—tears in her eyes—how on April 15, 1944, during the selection on the platform at Birkenau, little Emile Zuckerberg, a five-year-old who adored her, was torn from her arms by the SS and led to the gas chamber.

These children and their guardians, who had found a refuge in this French village, had only survival in mind. They in no way threatened the safety of the army of occupation. For the most part, these children had already suffered terrible misfortunes— among them, separation from their parents, who often had been deported after having been interned in the camps of the Free Zone, then handed spinelessly over by Vichy to the SS in the Occupied Zone. Meanwhile, the children had been rescued by organizations or by individuals—like Mrs. Zlatin, both dedicated and brave—who had snatched them out of Vichy's camps and were trying to save them from deportation.

All of them were Jews. Even if the monument erected in their memory does not say so. Even if the newspaper *Les Allobroges*, upon the inauguration of the memorial on April 7, 1946, wrote thus: "They faced the future with a smile. It took only a handful of brutes to reduce their hopes to nought. But why? Yes, one must ask oneself why. Because their parents were Jews? Because they were Communists? Or purely and simply Gaullists? All the same, that was no reason to murder the parents. Could it then have been a reason to murder the children themselves?"

According to the editorial page of the second local newspaper, *Le Coq Bugiste*, on this same April 6, 1946: "The Krauts would unquestionably have told you that the children were of terrorist stock, as their parents had been terrorists. Let that read 'patriots' and 'members of the Resistance'—perhaps Jews or Communists, with partisans besides, and natives of Alsace-Lorraine or foreigners."

The Jewish identity of these children has been restored to them bit by bit, and we have done our best to reconstruct their personal histories and the roads that led them to this house at Izieu, where the racial hatred of Nazis plunged headlong into the hunt for Jews was to strike them all down at once.

For nearly thirteen years, I have been living with the children of Izieu, who furnished the underlying motive for our efforts to find, expose, and bring to trial the man who, in ordering their arrest, had condemned them to death.

Mrs. Benguigui lost her three boys, Jacques, Richard, and Jean-Claude; she struggled bravely beside my wife, Beate, in Munich in 1971. The valiant Mrs. Halaunbrenner lost her two daughters, Mina and Claudine; she campaigned with Beate in La Paz. We salute these two mothers, as heroines and as martyrs. They are the incarnation of the "Jewish mother" in all her dignity. It is to them that we promised to ignore the limits of the possible in order to put an end to the freedom of their children's tormentor....The mothers of other children from Izieu are still alive, and suffer unendingly from the crime committed here against these Jewish children, and against all humanity.

Klaus Barbie. Left, above and below: Photographs dating from the early years of the war, possibly 1940. The photographs opposite, taken when Barbie was imprisoned briefly after the war in occupied Germany's American Zone, bear the date July 23, 1948. It is not known whether this was the date on which the photographs were taken or the date on which they were transmitted to the French police.

BARBIE UNPUNISHED

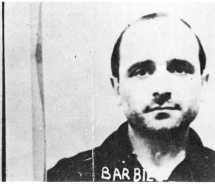

Ⅰn the *Who's Who* of Nazi criminals, Klaus Barbie is far from the most prominent name. It fell not to him to settle upon the Final Solution or to organize it in all its scope, as it did to Reinhard Heydrich or to Adolf Eichmann. He did not rule over a concentration camp, as did Rudolf Höss. He did not carry out the "selection" of scores of thousands of deportees, nor conduct monstrous "medical" experiments, as did Josef Mengele. He had no share in the responsibilities of administering the Nazi police force for an entire occupied country, as did Oberg, Knochen, Lischka, and Hagen in France. He perfected no technical means of mass murder, such as the mobile gas chambers of Walter Rauff. Barbie is not a member of the board of directors of the Nazi crime, but a middle manager. He is the very symbol of the Gestapo as it raged in our land. The higher-ups of the Nazi police had no contact with their victims; they acted through their Barbies. It was Barbie himself who left a palpable memory with those of his prisoners who survived. He was a particularly zealous and fanatical local operative.

Barbie both ordered up torture and applied it himself; and it is thus that his name has become indissolubly linked with that most celebrated of Resistance men, Jean Moulin, who, withstanding all efforts to make him talk, finally died from the treatment he received at Barbie's hands. Moulin's renown has only grown with time—as has that of his torturer, who as head of the Lyon Gestapo was behind a profusion of summary mass executions and who, even as the hour of defeat drew near, refused to spare the many prisoners at Fort Montluc, Resistance workers and Jews whom he was no longer in a position to deport.

Klaus Barbie not only arrested and tortured Moulin, he also, with full intent, put an end to the lives of more than forty Jewish children—children who posed no threat to the German authorities and who, having found refuge at Izieu, were seeking only to be forgotten, and to survive. When he cabled, on April 6, 1944, of the successful liquidation of this home for Jewish children between the ages of three and thirteen, Barbie signed his name to a crime whose infamy has grown with the years. Barbie's telegram, cited at Nuremberg as evidence of the anti-Jewish crimes committed in France, has entered into history, proof of a ruthlessness that in intensity—and in absolute evil—outstripped that which was loosed against the Resistance.

It is for these children—and for those of their mothers who are still alive and who, like Mrs. Halaunbrenner and Mrs. Benguigui, have suffered so long—that we decided to prevent Barbie from being whitewashed in Germany, and to track him down, unmask him, and have him brought to trial. Barbie, by his very position with the Gestapo, could have closed his eyes to the presence of these children in the territory under his command. Certain Gestapo chiefs did just that; apart from the Paris children's homes of the UGIF, liquidated in July 1944 by Alois Brunner, such centers were either forgotten or spared.

Our goal has long been the conviction in Germany of high-echelon officers like Lischka and Hagen, as well as of Barbie and Brunner. My wife, Beate, located Barbie in La Paz in 1971, I found Brunner in Damascus in 1982—and we did not hesitate to denounce these criminals on the spot. Beate was moved to action by the unjust loss of these young lives, prematurely snuffed out by the anti-Jewish hatred of Klaus Barbie.

We do not know whether the memory of these children calls out for vengeance. But we were sure that it demanded that Barbie not remain unpunished. For his is an exceptional impunity; it was secured by the American Special Services, which had employed this former Gestapo agent, then washed its hands of him by shipping him off to South America. Exposed, through our efforts, in 1972, Barbie remained at large for more than ten years under the protection of the Bolivian dictator, Colonel Hugo Banzer, and his successors. But despite this flight to the other side of the world, and despite the passage of time, the long arm of justice has finally fallen upon Barbie, bringing him back to the scene of his crimes and astonishing those—a very large majority—who no longer believed, or who never had believed, that such would come to pass.

From Barbie's trial, one should expect no revelations; the Gestapo's name has already been made. Rather, his trial is a necessary act, an act which will finally close a chapter marked by great suffering, suffering that continues even today for so many families.

Some of the children and their guardians, at Izieu in the summer of 1943.

THE RESCUE OF JEWISH CHILDREN BY OSE

The tragedy of Izieu must be viewed against the background of the rescue of thousands of Jewish children. One of a number of Jewish organizations that distinguished themselves in these endeavors was OSE,* which succeeded through both legal and covert means in liberating children from Vichy internment camps, sheltering them, and saving them from deportation. The home for children at Izieu, though not under OSE's direct supervision, was nonetheless closely tied to the organization, and OSE paid out a stipend for each of the children at Izieu. For this reason, we include extensive excerpts from a report on the activity of OSE that constitutes a chapter in *L'Activité des Organisations Juives en France sous l'Occupation* (The activities of Jewish organizations in France under the occupation), published in 1946 by the Jewish Contemporary Documentation Center in Paris.

On the eve of World War II, in consequence of the wave of Jewish emigrants from Germany, Austria, and Czechoslovakia who had been pouring into France in the late 1930s, OSE was lodging some three hundred young refugees at five children's homes in the Paris suburbs. When France declared war on Germany in September 1939, OSE's board—uncertain of the course the war would take and anxious to spare the children a hasty evacuation—began looking for homes in central France to use as fall-back positions. Six such homes, opened between November 1939 and March 1940, were at first occupied almost exclusively by children whose families had fled Paris. In June 1940, amid the panic that attended the French collapse, children from the homes in the Paris region were evacuated—the last of

them only a day before German troops entered the French capital—and sprinkled among the OSE homes in central France, whose number had grown to nine.

But OSE soon found itself responsible not only for the refugee children from Central Europe and for those whose parents had fled Paris or gone into hiding, but also for children whose parents had been taken prisoner of war or placed in internment camps. No longer able to confine itself to health care, OSE set up a network of institutions that provided social as well as medical services, organized aid to internees in camps, and began child-rescue operations.

In June 1940, OSE moved its headquarters to Vichy in the Free Zone, while still maintaining an office in Paris; soon thereafter, the headquarters were moved again, this time to Montpellier, where they remained until November 1942, when the Germans extended their occupation to the south of France.

June 1940–August 1942

Occupied Zone

OSE's first task was to rescue those refugee children who had not been in its homes, and had thus not been evacuated before the armistice and partition of France. The clandestine transfer of children into the Free Zone to the south—and in many cases on into neutral Switzerland—was a constant OSE activity. OSE also assisted families that stayed together, even arranging for the celebration of Jewish holidays.

OSE's task became more difficult following a decree, issued in July 1942, ordering Jews to wear the yellow star and banning them from parks and other public places. Nonetheless, children were taken for walks, and special movie screenings were arranged for them.

Free Zone

Benefiting from conditions less difficult than in the Occupied Zone, OSE established an extensive system of social-medical centers, which it located in Marseilles, Lyon, Grenoble, Mont-

OSE, pronounced "ozay," is a preventive health care organization founded in Russia by Jewish physicians in 1912. Its headquarters moved to Berlin shortly after the Russian Revolution, then on to Paris when the Nazis took power in Germany in 1933. An American branch of OSE, opened around the beginning of World War II, joined in efforts to bring Jewish children from wartime France to the United States. OSE is now based in Israel and has most recently been active there and in North Africa, running mobile clinics and providing other medical and social welfare services. The acronym OSE is derived from the organization's original Russian name and seems to have inspired its name in French, "Oeuvre de Secours aux Enfants" (Children's Welfare Organization).

Deportation by Convoy

	no. 71 April 13	no. 72 April 20	no. 73 May 15	no. 74 May 20	no. 75 May 30	no. 76 June 30
The 44 Children	34		2	2	3	3
The 7 Adults	4	1	1			1

Age	Number of Children
4	1
5	5
6	1
7	2
8	7
9	3
10	9
11	3
12	6
13	4
14	0
15	1
16	1
17	1

Country of Origin	Number of Children
France	21 (of which 7 were from Algeria)
Belgium	8
Germany	7
Austria	7
Poland	1

Of the 44 children, 17 had both parents deported, 12 had their fathers deported, and 10 had their mothers deported.

pellier, Perigueux, Toulouse, Limoges, Nice, and Chambéry, as well as in a number of smaller towns.

The first of these centers, at Marseilles, was opened in June 1941 with the aid of the Unitarian Service Committee. Provided with medical and dental clinics, as well as laboratory facilities, it owed its importance both to the presence of refugees who streamed into this port city and to its proximity to the internment camp at Les Milles. Lyon, the first OSE center to engage in clandestine activity, was opened in November 1941; it began issuing false identity papers to foreign Jews—the first in France to whom anti-Jewish measures were applied—as early as April 1942. Limoges became an important center due to the hospitable attitude of the local populace in general and the authorities in particular. Montpellier was the site not only of OSE's headquarters, but, from March 1941, of a social-medical center as well.

Through regular visits to families, above all to children; through consultations on medical problems and systematic health checks; through substantial aid, both in currency and in kind; through a specialized placement service covering spas and sanatoria; through the meticulous organization of hospitalization and convalescent periods; through the proliferation of institutions for supplementing and extending health-care activities, such as day nurseries, cantines, and social clubs; and through its ceaseless contact with administrative bodies, the public-service role OSE played in the life of the Jewish communities grew daily.

Despite the dispersion of the refugee families—in remote villages, on isolated farms—OSE's message of concern and protection reached them all; taking a thousand different forms, it was carried to the most out-of-the-way and inaccessible places by a young and enthusiastic team braving all weather and employing any means at hand. The cohesion and vigor of its actions were due, in large part, to close and continuous cooperation within OSE, which was, in itself, a social achievement of the first order.

More than five thousand families, foreign and French, and more than four thousand children benefited in varying degrees from OSE's manifold activities. Giving the same scrupulous attention to specific tasks as to the implementation of broad strategies, OSE succeeded, even in the precarious conditions of the time, in turning its activities into a kind of social insurance scheme that allowed it to limit, up to a point, the number of future victims.

In the fall of 1940, the Vichy government set up camps in which it interned Jews who had been deported by Germany from their homes in the Rhineland, who had fled Central Europe or the Low Countries for France, or who otherwise lacked French nationality. Conditions were abominable: unprotected from the elements, inadequately fed and clothed, obliged to drink impure water, prey to vermin and infectious diseases, living in filth and enforced inactivity, three thousand internees—some fifteen percent of the total camp populations—perished in these camps.

From the very beginning, OSE workers took up residence in the camps, setting up medical facilities, child-welfare centers, social clubs, even libraries. In some cases, they succeeded in having accommodations disinfected, sanitation improved, and glass panes placed in barracks windows. They managed to provide dietary supplements, particularly for the sick. They coordinated the work of the various organizations, Jewish and non-Jewish alike, that had representatives in the camps, helped obtain legal assistance, and won permission for some internees to spend short periods at liberty in nearby towns.

In addition, following repeated approaches to Vichy authorities—and thanks to the sympathetic posture of some among them—OSE was able, between November 1941 and May 1942, to procure the official release of more than one thousand children under the age of fifteen and of many fifteen and over as well.

Jewish children from OSE's home at Palavas-les-Flots, near Montpellier on the Mediterranean coast. The photograph dates from 1942.

In order to be released from the camps, children were required to be in possession of a residence permit authorized by the prefect of the department in which they were to be lodged. We must pay a grateful tribute to the prefect of the department of Hérault, to his secretary general, and to his chief of staff, who, at a time when few officials were so disposed, found a way to reconcile their station as civil servants with their consciences as human beings. It was owing to the courage of these individuals whose patriotism was not besmirched by the orders of Vichy, and to that of OSE Secretary General Joseph Millner, whose efforts in saving children proved particularly fruitful, that children awaiting release from the camps had access to residence certificates for Hérault.

Thus, Montpellier, Hérault's departmental seat, became the locus of efforts to liberate children from internment by legal means, and the surrounding region saw the creation of numerous "vacation camps," which in reality were designed to provide increased security for the placing of these children. In the summer of 1941, a shelter for legally liberated children was set up at Palavas-les-Flots, on the Mediterranean coast near Montpellier; it soon became a veritable switching yard, a way station through which the children, restored to liberty, passed en route to homes under the jurisdiction of OSE's Montpellier social-medical center. And once the children's status had been made legal in

Hérault, it was easy to shift them to other departments, because moving those under the age of fifteen did not require any additional formalities.

In a similar way—through an oversight, whether intentional or inadvertent, at the prefecture in Perpignan—it became possible to liberate a large number of adolescents fifteen and older. These were sheltered, for the most part, by the EIF (Eclaireurs Israélites de France, or Jewish Boy Scouts of France), an organization that played an active role in the Resistance.

However, before such channels had been established and recognized, how many fruitless attempts had been made; how many dossiers carefully assembled only to go astray; how many desperate approaches dared to indifferent, even hostile bureaucrats who had apparently been won over to the "New European Order"?

As early as July 1940, some who had left their children under OSE's care as they fled the German advance were weighing a return to the north; but as these parents began taking their children out of the homes, others, fearful of what the occupation might bring, were putting theirs in. Moreover, throughout this period, children who had been released from the camps arrived to swell the ranks. Faced with this deluge, OSE could not afford to be strict about the number of children the homes could accommo-

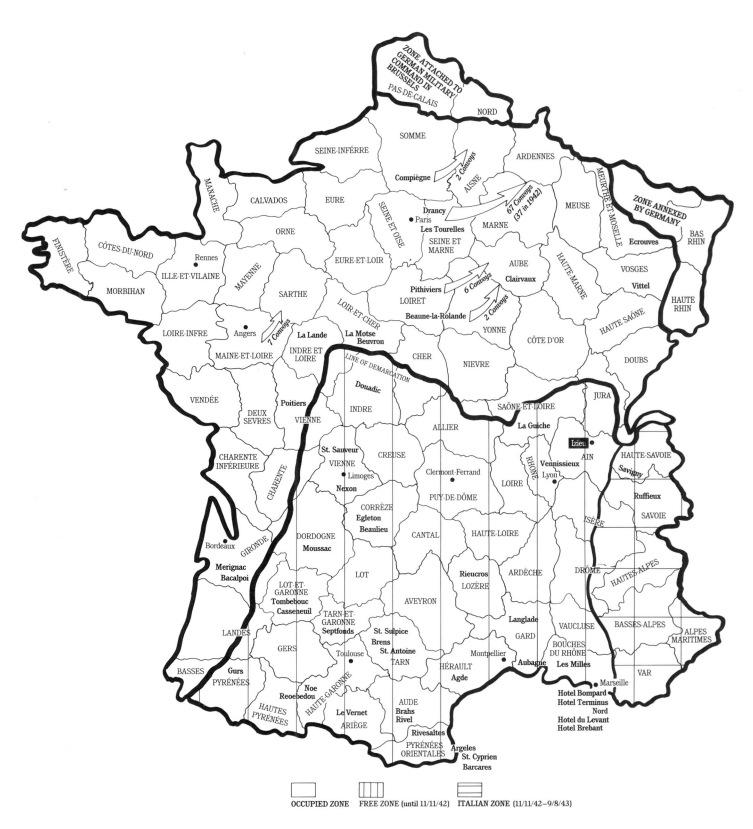

France in 1942–44. The map shows the Line of Demarcation and the location of some of the principal internment camps.

OCCUPIED ZONE **FREE ZONE** (until 11/11/42) **ITALIAN ZONE** (11/11/42–9/8/43)

date, although it was ultimately obliged to remove some children to foster households or educational institutions, and to place other children with them directly. Thus, families and schools gradually complemented the homes.

OSE did everything it could to make its own institutions true homes rather than mere receiving stations, but given the coming and going of children of different backgrounds it was next to impossible to assign sleeping quarters according to age or to provide a thoroughly organized communal life. Nonetheless, staff shortages were overcome by the addition of young women from the Jewish youth movements—many of whom had arrived in France shortly before the war—as nurses and social workers; teachers and doctors who had been dismissed under Vichy's anti-Jewish measures also came to work in the homes. Vocational training did much to combat the unrest caused among the children by the general atmosphere of alarm; sports were added at the end of 1941; and great emphasis was placed on Jewish education, which took different forms in the different homes and ranged from instruction in Jewish tradition and sociology to Palestine discussion groups. By 1942 there were fourteen OSE homes, housing over one thousand children in all. The care provided the children was such that the OSE homes have remained for some among the happiest memories of the period of occupation.

I n conjunction with the American Joint Distribution Committee, the American Friends Service Committee, and its own United States branch, OSE succeeded, early in 1941, in obtaining three hundred American visas for Jewish children in France. The visas were earmarked for children interned at the Gurs and Rivesaltes camps; once these children had been released and placed in OSE homes, representatives of OSE and the Friends visited the homes to select those who, in line with American stipulations, were under sixteen and in excellent health.

Preparation for the three departures—in May 1941, August 1941, and May 1942—was long and exacting. Parents being held in internment camps submitted declarations to OSE authorizing their children's departure, passage for the children and the OSE workers accompanying them was booked, and those who had been chosen were brought to Marseilles and put up in an OSE home there. If the first two groups left amid relative calm, the third was organized in an atmosphere of extreme anxiety, and set sail just before communications with the United States were broken off.

In the summer of 1942, the United States Committee for the Care of European Children, which had arranged to sponsor these children when they reached America, obtained an additional thousand visas. Children were selected quickly, and a number were already in Marseilles awaiting passage when, in November, the Allies landed in North Africa. Prevented from sailing, the children were interned; after great effort, they were ultimately released.

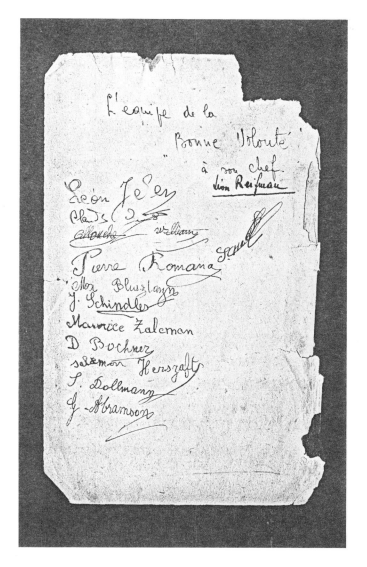

Top: Before his residence at Izieu, Léon Reifman (center) was a counselor for these children at Palavas-les Flots. Above: A list of the children in Reifman's group, written in their own hands.

August 1942–February 1944

The work of the preceding period can be characterized as legal, particularly in the Free Zone, but its legality was relative at best. The incorporation of OSE into the UGIF-South, ordered by the Commissariat-General for Jewish Affairs in March 1942, only

heightened the split between the front activities tolerated by the Vichy government and OSE's true mission: the physical and spiritual preservation of the Jewish population. The severity of those in power, coupled with their acknowledged objectives, pushed OSE officials toward laying the foundation for an underground network that would not be shackled as regulations grew increasingly draconian.

The wave of roundups, arrests, and deportations aimed at foreign Jews in the months of July and August 1942 confirmed the gloomiest of expectations. Carried out by a police force that was cowardly, servile, and no stranger to dirty work, these arrests spread rapidly from the Occupied to the Free Zone. The sinister names of Gurs, Rivesaltes, Les Milles, Drancy, Pithiviers, Vénissieux, Nexon, and Beaune-la-Rolande will forever live in human memory as a reminder of the savagery of the Nazis, of the right of asylum flouted, of the shame of hospitality betrayed. May they deflect the humanity of tomorrow from any like abyss.

In the face of this open season on humans, decreed by the German Moloch and conducted by its lackeys, the lives of the refugee population were thrown into utter disarray. A new pattern of migration made its appearance, but whereas the initial flights had tended to follow the problematic roads to safety from east to west and from north to south, this latest disregarded even the most elementary rules. Jews from the cities fanned out into the countryside, and those in the country flooded toward the towns. Reason was no longer their guide.

The German move into the previously unoccupied South Zone in November 1942 destroyed whatever illusions remained. Henceforward, police operations would be coordinated throughout the entire country; immediately, the German police ordered posted in each prefecture a list of the foreign Jews residing in the department. The result was a panic of unprecedented proportions, and a new round of migration occurred, this time to the zone of Italian occupation in the southeast. Those who reached the Italian zone enjoyed rule that was incomparably more merciful than in the German zone, and in general were under no heavier restriction than assigned residence in a given town. Many others, however, fell victim to the Germans when they were snared along the way.

From one day to the next, problems that had seemed essential faded into the background, while totally new tasks cropped up. The chief matter at hand was saving the lives of the persecuted, starting with the children. Fully aware of its responsibilities in the face of a situation unlike any the world had ever seen, OSE called once again upon the acumen of its directorate and the heroic self-sacrifice of its rank and file in coming to grips with the new and onerous duties that had been reserved for them by destiny.

North Zone

The major roundup of July 1942, in which women and children were arrested for the first time, marked a turning point. From then on, the principal task of OSE—as of other Jewish organizations—was to save the maximum number of both children and adults by placing them in hiding.

To provide an indispensable contact point for the growing number of parents who wanted their children hidden, OSE set up an office in a tiny room in Paris, under the guise of a social club. The children who visited this "club" were placed with Christian families; OSE workers stayed in constant touch with the children and their guardians, ensuring that allowance payments were made on time and keeping as strict an accounting as possible. In close cooperation with other Jewish organizations and with non-Jewish individuals and bodies who, unsolicited, provided many forms of aid, OSE was able not only to place the children but also, when necessary, to provide false identity papers and ration coupons to children and adults alike.

The number of children continued to climb, and the work became increasingly difficult and dangerous, but OSE's staff held out courageously to the end. Although its activities were scattered around Paris and carefully disguised, and although its documents—camouflaged to avoid leaving the slightest clue—were to be found sometimes here, sometimes there, the staff worked such wonders that after the liberation it was able to account for the most minute expenditure. In all, some seven hundred children were successfully hidden in the North Zone through the good offices of OSE.

Serge Klarsfeld and his sister Georgette were in the OSE children's home Château de Masgelier in the department of Creuse in central France. Their father, Arno Klarsfeld a member of the Corps of Foreign Volunteers of the French Army, escaped from a German POW camp; he then took his children out of the home and brought them to Nice. After having placed in hiding—and thereby saved—his wife and two children, Arno Klarsfeld was arrested in Nice and deported. Opposite: Serge and Georgette with their father, wearing a French Army jacket. Right: Children from the Château de Masgelier, including Georgette (right background), with Arno Klarsfeld. Both photographs were taken in 1941 in front of the château.

South Zone

After years of running the most varied institutions and of bringing constructive action to all its fields of endeavor, OSE was obliged, when the German occupation was extended to the south of France in November 1942, to contemplate, on short notice, a radical revision of the manner in which it conceived and organized its work. In particular, it was now imperative to disperse groups that were in danger in order to shield their members from certain persecution. In the words of wise King Solomon, it was no longer "a time to build up," but "a time to break down."

While OSE's framework of children's homes and social-medical centers was in fact maintained, what went on inside them gradually changed. Where formerly the sick had been treated, instruction lavished, and assistance meted out, there now appeared dens that organized clandestine border crossings, laboratories turning out false identity papers, and hideouts where fugitives could hole up—all with the sole objective of protecting children from the enemy.

The first measures taken by OSE were aimed at aiding the victims of mass arrests. Capitalizing on the official status of the organization, social workers slipped into the assembly points and selection centers. There they made sure provisions were supplied to the internees and observed screening procedures; they also attempted to forestall by legal means the deportation of those whose cases could be pleaded before the authorities, and by illegal means the deportation of those who had a chance of escape. But in the majority of cases no intercession was possible, and OSE workers could do no more than accompany the hapless victims to the Line of Demarcation, comforting them and receiving in trust their last requests.

In almost every instance, these wishes concerned their children; for, by an inexplicable stroke of luck—which, before long, would be no more than a fond memory—those under the age of sixteen were allowed to stay in France at the time of the first deportations. Children who lived in danger of being left alone, and others already on their own, sought assistance and protection. OSE, in conjunction with such organizations as the EIF, the Friends, the YMCA, the Swiss welfare agency Secours Suisse, and Amitié Chrétienne, a nondenominational Christian group that was extremely active in underground work, set up a courageous emergency program to feed, clothe, and shelter the entirety of these imperiled young.

In the wake of massive roundups that hit Marseilles in January 1943, OSE began organizing escape routes and supply lines to the countryside. Adults by the hundreds were armed with false papers on the very premises of the OSE dispensary, where social-welfare and medical activities were now no more than a facade. At the same time, groups comprised of both children and adults began leaving in the direction of Switzerland, guided by OSE workers in close liaison with the EIF and other organizations; almost every week, groups of children were accompanied from Marseilles, Nice, and Aix-en-Provence to the Swiss border.

Around the same time, OSE operations in Lyon suffered their first losses. During a Gestapo raid on the Lyon offices of UGIF on February 9, 1943, two OSE medical workers, Dr. Pierre Lanzenberg and Marcelle Loeb, were arrested. Other workers were obliged to go underground.

Though reduced in number, the Lyon staff managed not only to maintain OSE's principal activities in that city, but to expand its programs in Grenoble and to get work underway in Chambéry, where from February 1943 the organization was headquartered. Owing to the more favorable conditions in the Italian-occupied zone, the Grenoble and Chambéry centers rapidly gained in importance. Many foreign Jews whose legal status was irregular were able to find a stable residence in a town or village of the region, and thus to enjoy a respite from flight.

However, in September 1943 the Germans moved into the Italian zone, and panic ensued. Jews rushed en masse to Nice, where, according to rumor, the Italian occupation was to be maintained—and all those who were unable to leave clamored for false papers. Once again, parents entrusted their children to OSE, which stepped up its clandestine work.

Whether in the zone previously occupied by the Italians or in the German-occupied zone, conditions worsened by the day. In response to the many acts of sabotage that took place around Grenoble, the Germans staged raids, mass arrests, house searches, and executions. The OSE office was raided twice by the Gestapo, in November 1943 and January 1944; ultimately, OSE was obliged to leave the city.

As the general situation deteriorated, so did conditions in the camps. In August 1942, when OSE learned from a confidential report that ten thousand inmates from the internment camps in the South Zone were to be handed over for deportation, messengers were dispatched to Gurs and Rivesaltes. They found that Vichy had ordered releases stopped. Claims for exemption were accepted on behalf of those over sixty; the parents of children under the age of two; Hungarian, Rumanian, and Turkish nationals; aliens who had resided in France since 1935 or before; and those who had served in the French armed forces, with their immediate families. Not all claims were admitted, however, and some of the grounds for exemption were withdrawn in subsequent weeks.

OSE representatives were nonetheless able to have many deportations deferred; in the interval, they supplied those in question with false identity papers and, working with the underground section of the EIF, helped them to escape. They provided aid to those who remained inside the camps as well and, when there was no more that could be done, took messages to their relatives and friends. The courage and confidence the OSE workers' presence inspired in the internees is impossible to overstate.

The tragic events of August 1942 affected the OSE staff in Marseilles before those in other cities, as Les Milles became, in the first days of the month, the central point of assembly and transport for the entire south of France. It is hardly possible to recount the drama of the days, of the long nights of selection, of the departure by cattle car in the first light of dawn, or—foremost and always—of the heart-rending cries that accompanied them. Nor is it possible to put into words what went on in the souls of the OSE team as they led away some one hundred children and adolescents whom, in an all-out struggle, they had wrested from confinement before the eyes of parents who were never to see them again.

On August 18, Vénissieux and Fort-Paillet, near to Lyon, became assembly and selection points for foreign Jews who had been placed under arrest. Two days later, workers from the OSE center in Lyon, in cooperation with representatives of non-Jewish organizations, brought about the release from Vénissieux of 108 children, whom they immediately placed with families.

OSE workers took advantage of the confusion that reigned in the camps to wage inch-by-inch battles for the children with their jailers. On some occasions, albeit rare ones, the jailers fought back: the regional prefect at Lyon demanded, for the purpose of "family reunification," the return of the children rescued from Vénissieux. But despite his vigorous insistence, his efforts were in vain.

Everywhere, the liberation of children was the object of a combat that consumed every day, every hour, fought with unequal arms but sustained with an ardor that was never wanting. The adventures, the strokes of luck, the wonders of the imagination to which these rescues gave rise would be too many to enumerate here. Still, it would be worthwhile to enter into the record how a group of boys over sixteen managed to escape from Les Milles by climbing onto a roof, where for four days they hid behind a water tank and were fed by a valiant cook. Or how Andrée Salomon succeeded in applying the normal procedure for release—even though it was strictly prohibited—to children at Rivesaltes whose parents were, at the time, unwilling to be separated from them. Or how a woman of courage and great heart like Mary Elms slipped out of Rivesaltes some thirty young children for whom no official release had been granted. Or how, after the tragic events of August 20—when the first train leaving Rivesaltes carried, in addition to nine hundred adults, eighty-two children between two and eighteen years old—the OSE staff, battling to the last ounce of their strength, won exemption for twenty imperiled children. Or how a clever bit of playacting on the part of a fraudulent representative of the Swiss Red Cross allowed another twenty-five of the six hundred children freed from Rivesaltes to be sneaked away.

In addition, OSE set up special barracks for children so that it could supplement their rations and remove them from the overcrowding that plagued the adults. And there would be much to say about the atmosphere that reigned there as well: about the moving scenes attending the separations; about the concern even the youngest children showed for their parents, whom they knew

Front view of the house at Izieu as it looks today. At right, above flower box, is the commemorative plaque.

to be in danger; about the boy who, every day, brought to his father half of his soup; about the little girl who could hardly be prevented from climbing after her mother into the truck that was to cover the first leg of her deportation; about their rejection of all delight—in a word, about the precocity with which the children went about attending to their parents' physical existence and their own once they understood that, from then on, they would be left to fend for themselves.

The OSE children's homes were an unexpected target for the waves of persecution, but what an easy target they made. Beginning in late August 1942, French gendarmes and military police encircled the homes, arresting children sixteen and over who were of German, Austrian, Czech, and Polish origin; many of these children had come to France to escape the Nazis, and had been raised in the homes. Younger children whose parents were in the camps were also picked up, on the hypocritical pretext of reuniting families—before sending them off to their deaths. Official steps were taken immediately, and the children under sixteen were released. With few exceptions, however, the rest remained in the camps and met the general fate.

As the Gestapo and Milice became more active in central France, some of the older children were moved to the Italian-occupied zone. But the new homes established there were not to last. Upsetting all expectations, Italy capitulated, opening the border regions to the Gestapo's criminal activity and making the homes there just as precarious—if not more so—than those in the center of the country.

Uneasy at keeping so many Jewish children in the same place, OSE tried to thin out homes that were overcrowded. But no sooner would a few beds be freed than other children would be delivered by their panicking families into OSE's custody. The constant coming and going; the heartbreaking scenes in the presence of the young wards; the daily reports of the parents' deportation; the raids by the police; the difficulties to which the staff members themselves fell prey: all contributed to keeping the children in a state of distress and to creating an atmosphere of nervous tension detrimental to their development. It is not the least of the OSE staffs' achievements that, though exposed to constant risk, they continued to lead courses and seminars, workshops and games, enveloping the children in a sphere of quiet and calm.

Shutting down the homes, dispersing the children, and putting an end to OSE's official activities was seriously considered on numerous occasions. No longer places of refuge, the homes had become booby traps. Only the fact that it would have been impossible to make nearly a thousand children disappear overnight compelled OSE to postpone these radical decisions.

From the summer of 1943, an OSE underground network was active throughout the South Zone, with the exception of the coastal areas; by the end of the year, 1,600 children were in its charge. The network had a central office in Lyon under the direction of Georges Garel, a Resistance man known for his daring, who had been brought into OSE to set up its clandestine operations. In addition, there were four regional bureaus: the East Central, also in Lyon, run by Victor Svarc—known as "Souvard"—and responsible for 350 children; the Central, in Limoges, run by Edith Scheftel—known as both "Jacqueline Estager" and "Pauline Gaudefroi"—with 450 children; the Southeast, in Valence, run by Robert Ebstein and Fanny Loinger—"Evrard" and "Laugier"—with 400 children; and the Southwest, in Toulouse, run by Solange Zitlenok—"Rémy"—with 400 children. The organization of this new network was

guided by three main principles: dispersing the Jewish children in non-Jewish surroundings where no one knew them; providing each with an assumed "Aryan" identity; and entrusting the upkeep of these camouflage arrangements to personnel who were, or appeared to be, non-Jews.

The first to provide Garel with a precious gesture of encouragement had been the archbishop of Toulouse, Monsignor Jules-Gérard Saliège, and his coadjutor, Monsignor de Courrèges. Immediately upon being briefed, the archbishop—who had spoken from the pulpit against the discriminatory measures, the separation of families, and the deportations—threw his support to the project: he gave Garel a letter of introduction, which was to open many doors. Monsignor de Courrèges, himself later arrested and deported, helped arrange accommodations for the first twenty-four children who left their OSE foster families for Christian institutions. One need only consider the risk inherent in such actions and their inestimable value to understand the reverence and gratitude felt by the members of OSE's underground section toward these two men of the cloth.

Soon, the entire South Zone was being combed for Christian children's homes willing to take in Jewish children under false names. Contact was subsequently made with Protestant officials; the Reverend Rolland de Pury, before his own arrest, and the Reverend Marc Boegner, the leader of France's Protestants, lent their support as well. But not only the churches helped—valuable assistance came from people of every background and social class. And this outburst of solidarity, welling up in the French majority, allowed OSE to find in each diocese, in every department, institutions—religious or secular, public or private—that accepted and cared for Jewish children or acted as OSE's screen.

The first underground workers were women on OSE's staff who had been released by the closing of the homes. Various Christian institutions listed them as personnel under false identities, and Christian Resistance operatives soon began sharing their tasks as well. When it was certain that a given local institution would protect children—and that the workers' activities could be made to appear normal through the sanction of some departmental body—the staggered yet ever more frequent arrivals of children in search of refuge began.

The children, with whatever possessions they had, would travel in small groups under the supervision of a social worker or group leader, who would turn back after handing them over to the local operative. The latter would have them put up wherever possible until permanent accommodations could be found. Then the game would begin again, and other children, their eyes wide with astonishment, were brought along in the same way, to be spread far and wide among the families of farmers, craftsmen, laborers, teachers, and shopowners, or placed in institutions. When, as sometimes happened, a child's false identity broke down—whether through the fault of the child or of the guardian—he or she had to be removed immediately and placed elsewhere in order to avoid compromising all work that had been accomplished in the area.

The fabric of OSE's underground network involved other illegal operations as well. Hiding the children and disguising the staff called for extensive production and distribution of false identity papers; here, municipal employees and printers working with Resistance groups helped a great deal. OSE bureaus in Grenoble and Limoges coordinated the purchase and transport of clothing for the children; if caught, workers engaged in this extremely hazardous activity were to pass themselves off as black marketeers.

Both Jewish and non-Jewish organizations maintained a degree of coordination amongst themselves, and OSE made

Left: The house at Izieu as seen from the terrace, 1984. Opposite: In front of the house is a well ringed by a stone railing. The photograph at left was taken in 1944, the one at right in 1984.

arrangements ensuring that whatever happened, its work would be carried on. So that the children could be traced even in the event that all OSE workers disappeared, coded lists of names were compiled and sent to Geneva, where the organization had established an office in December 1942. From this base in neutral Switzerland, OSE was able to stay in touch with the outside world and to maintain steady contact with the headquarters in Chambéry, which proved of great help in the organization's clandestine work.

Throughout this entire period, foster families were in plentiful supply. In fact, the eagerness of Christian families to receive Jewish children was often most touching. Poor or well-to-do, urban or rural, rare was the family that, once approached, refused the charitable duty requested of it. Of course, families received an allowance plus supplementary expenses, but it became clear in hindsight that many foster parents would have cared for the children without any remuneration whatever, feeding and clothing them at their own expense. For their part, many children became attached to their foster parents, which occasioned difficulties after the liberation, when children were either returned to their real parents—those who had survived—or placed in Jewish children's homes where they could be brought up as Jews.

At the very height of the terror, OSE's board drew up a plan for smuggling children into neutral countries, the first and foremost of which was Switzerland. After long and meticulous preparation, this plan was put into operation in 1943. The Chambéry headquarters' delegate to the regional bureau at Limoges, Jenny Masour, worked with Robert Job and the directors of the various homes in selecting children to be transferred to new homes in the Italian zone or slipped across the Swiss border. Chosen for Switzerland were, in general, children whose typically "Jewish"

appearance or whose attachment to religious practice made them difficult to blend into a non-Jewish background—and thus whose safety in France could be little more than an illusion.

Groups of six to ten children, brought together in Grenoble or Chambéry and accompanied by guides working directly under OSE's orders, followed one another at regular intervals—and without incident—across the Swiss border. The pace was stepped up when the Italian occupation crumbled in September 1943; in fact, thanks to OSE representatives in the Italian zone, part of the adult Jewish population was also able to flee to Switzerland, thus escaping the piteous fate waiting in Nice for those who followed the retreating Italian forces. Beginning in August, two and sometimes three groups per week, each made up of twelve to twenty-five children, were led from Lyon to Aix-les-Bains and from there on to Annemasse. Following the Italian capitulation, German guards were positioned on the Franco-Swiss border: the crossings were immediately suspended, but within three months they resumed.

Escorted by Georges Loinger, the children made their way along the river Avre from the town of Annemasse to a wood close by, where a playing field had been marked out near the Swiss border. At dusk, following an afternoon of outdoor games during which they had forgotten entirely the danger to which they were exposed, the children crossed the border at a spot hidden by the woods and far from the nearest road or trail. Municipal officials from Annemasse helped immeasurably in these operations, as did a local partisan group, which sent out pickets to monitor German movements on crossing days. With danger on the rise, OSE called a halt to these border crossings two months before the liberation—but not before more than one thousand children had been smuggled out of harm's way.

Each perilous expedition was composed of many delicate

The children of Izieu in a photograph taken by a neighbor in March 1944.

phases—selection of the children, taken not only from institutions and foster families, but in some cases from their own families as well; preparation of the false papers allowing them to reach the frontier; instructions to be learned by heart; final baggage checks; organization and departure of the groups; accommodations for the numerous stops along the way; arrival in the border area; last-minute concealment of identity papers in the linings of clothes—plus a thousand and one secondary details, each of which had its importance. Then there was the crossing itself, by day or at night, to which those in charge, through their ingenuity and dedication, managed to impart the air of a holiday outing—but which could nevertheless dissolve, at any moment, into catastrophe.

All those who took part in activities of this nature will cherish the memory of Mila Racine, a young woman of twenty-four who was arrested in November 1943 when the group she was leading was surprised by the Germans. Deported to Germany, she would later perish in an air raid during the war's final days. Also belonging to the chronicle of unknown acts of heroism is the story of the last group of children to be captured at the Annemasse border. Georges Loinger and Emmanuel Racine, brother of Mila, managed to organize an escape for the group leader, Marianne Cohn, from the Hotel Pax, where she was being held with the children. However, she refused to abandon her charges. The children were later rescued, but Cohn—together with a partisan fighter and two other women—was shot down four days before the liberation.

A second, totally separate child-rescue operation was based in Nice. Correctly anticipating what might happen if the Germans took over the city, Moussa Abadi—aided by the bishop of Nice, Monsignor Rémond, and by Maurice Brener of the American Joint Distribution Committee—set up a vast network covering all of Nice and extending to Cannes and other towns in the region. With the close cooperation of OSE, whose social workers took the children from their families and placed them in this network's care, more than four hundred children were saved.

The OSE center itself played an important role in early rescue efforts in Nice. Scarcely hours after they had entered the city, the Germans were hunting down their human quarry with more ruthlessness and ferocity than had yet been seen. The sinister Alois Brunner left Drancy to direct the operation in person, and no one was spared, neither man nor woman nor child. The center's social and medical services could not be maintained; but in spite of the danger prowling at its gates OSE kept the center open. And it was there that parents whose hours were now numbered turned up seeking safety for their most precious of possessions: their children. An urgent call for reinforcements permitted some fifty children—most of whom were to find refuge in Switzerland—to escape Nice in the very midst of the round-ups. Within weeks, however, the Gestapo raided OSE offices, arresting and deporting all those found there.

Seeing each day's excesses outstripped on the morrow, OSE at last decided that in order to reduce the vulnerability of its operations and serve the best interests of the children it should evacuate its homes. But even as the children's homes feverishly prepared to shut their doors, OSE's social-medical centers continued functioning. For, in addition to those in the homes and in the underground network, more than one thousand children in families or institutions were under the care of the social-medical division.

And, beside those children for whom OSE alone was responsible, it aided close to fifteen hundred others living with their own families. Despite the problems arising from the extreme dispersion of these families and the risk entailed in each journey, OSE social workers succeeded in keeping the lines of assistance open. In fact, although everything might have prompted them to give up, they expanded their services, principally through increasing aid to adults. These workers were acutely aware that, at a time when resources were lacking, it was crucial to build up the physical and emotional staying power of their charges, whatever the cost.

OSE handed the homes it had closed over to local authorities or other institutions in an effort to cover the children's tracks and safeguard the facilities. When the evacuation of several homes was delayed, OSE found itself obliged to curtail its activities until the safety of the last children could be assured.

The terrace of the house at Izien, 1984.

This period of marking time was brought to a brutal conclusion on February 8, 1944, when the Gestapo raided OSE headquarters in Chambéry, arresting several staff members and numerous visitors. All the offices and social-medical centers were thereupon closed down, and OSE's legal activities came to an end.

February–September 1944

Sensing that they were losing the war, the Germans vented their rage on the civilian population, staging raids throughout the country, taking hostages, and leaving people dead in the streets. The persecution of Jews, always reserved a place of honor by the Nazis, went hand in hand with that of patriots, Resistance fighters, and those evading forced labor service in Germany. At the same time, the Resistance movement became bolder; German detachments were frequently attacked in the countryside, and German troop and supply trains were blown up daily.

The list of OSE casualties lengthened during this period, due in part to a series of arrests in May. Francis Chirat, a Christian social worker in close contact with OSE, was arrested in Lyon. Gertrude Blumenstock-Lévy was burned alive in a village the Germans set on fire. Julien Samuel and Jacques Salon saved themselves by jumping from the train that was taking them to Drancy. Dr. René Bloch, Eve Cahen, Marcel Geismar, and Robert Weill were all deported; only Weill survived deportation, returning to France after the end of the war.

The terrace at Izieu during the summer of 1943. Léa Feldblum, the only survivor among those arrested at Izieu and deported, can be seen in the center of the second row.

THE HOUSE AT IZIEU

"Settlement for Refugee Children from Hérault"

OSE's child-rescue operations played a major role in the creation of the refuge for Jewish children at Izieu.

As already mentioned, the center OSE had opened during the summer of 1941 at Palavas-les-Flots served for more than a year as a stopover point for children whose release had been won through legal channels. However, once the Free Zone had been taken over by the Germans in November 1942, OSE closed down this center, which had become too conspicuous, and founded or helped to found "vacation camps" designed to provide increased security for the work of placing children.

One of the main figures in the evacuation of Palavas-les-Flots was Sabina Zlatin. Born Sabina Chwast on January 13, 1907, in Warsaw, Mrs. Zlatin was a French Red Cross nurse who had procured a volunteer position as social worker for the department of Hérault, to which she and her husband, Miron, a distinguished agronomist, had fled from the northern tip of France. At her own request, Mrs. Zlatin was assigned to visit the camps of Agde and Rivesaltes, where families with children under fourteen were among the internees. At great risk to herself, she managed to get numerous children out of these camps. OSE, with which she was in close contact, was then able to place these children in its homes, smuggle them into Switzerland, or even arrange their emigration to the United States, with the help of the Quakers.

Toward the end of 1942, however, Mrs. Zlatin was advised by the prefecture of Hérault—one of the few departments whose officials took a benevolent stance toward the Jews—to leave the German zone for the more hospitable Italian zone, where the military authorities protected Jews against the intrigues of the Vichy police.

Taking with her the majority of the children from Palavas-les-Flots, Mrs. Zlatin left for Chambéry, where the Secours National, a state-run relief organization, provided shelter for all at a small hotel. Meanwhile, her husband accompanied some of the older children, Théo Reis and Paul Niederman among them, to OSE's center at Vic-sur-Cére, near the city of Aurillac in south-central France.

Léon Reifman, a medical student who had been a counselor at Palavas and was assisting Mrs. Zlatin, tried to scatter the children among religious institutions—the safest course—but his efforts were to no avail. So Mrs. Zlatin herself, again upon the recommendation of her friends at the Hérault prefecture, entered into contact with the thirty-three-year-old subprefect at Belley, Marcel Wiltzer, and with Marie-Antoinette Cojean, twenty-nine, the subprefecture's secretary general. They proposed a large house in nearby Izieu, a village set in a chain of mountains towering above the Rhone River valley; the house had been standing empty except during summer vacations, when it was used for children from a Catholic school. The offer was accepted, and, as a cover, this Jewish home was officially named "Settlement for Refugee Children from Hérault."

When OSE closed its home at Campestre à Lodéve near Montpellier toward the end of March 1943, the children of that center—some of whom had been at Palavas—and a few of their counselors made for the Italian zone. They met up with Mrs. Zlatin as she was taking over the house at Izieu, and other children were also beginning to arrive, either through OSE's underground network or directly from the OSE bureau in Lyon.

The home was under the supervision of Mrs. Zlatin and her husband, who had quickly joined her there; a stipend for each child was granted by OSE. Miron Zlatin, who handled the house finances, was, in the words of a neighbor, "a robust fellow who could ride up the hill pulling a hundred kilos in the trailer behind his bike." This neighbor, a Mr. Favet, added about the Zlatins, "those kids were their life."

One can get a glimpse of how the children lived from the letters and pictures reproduced alongside the individual profiles. But let us add here some notes from the letters of little Georges Halpern to his parents. From him, we know that the children had cocoa with bread and jam at breakfast, and milk with their bread and jam for snacks. Again thanks to him, we know that they took a nap every afternoon; that they had a dog; and that, at the end of winter, there was "no more snow. All the snow has melted. The weather is great, with a lot of sunshine. We go for hikes on Thursdays and Sundays." And he tells us that in class the children worked on "compositions, arithmetic, science, geography....I am in the elementary class, I'm third among eight, I scored sixty-four and a half. I have a composition book, a blue blotter, a fountain pen, a lead pencil, some colored crayons." We know, too, that there was a big party on Mardi Gras.*

*Mentioning in letters the names of Jewish holidays—in this case, most likely Purim—might have led to denunciation of the home; it may also have been prudent, for the sake of appearances, to hold celebrations on Christian holidays.

At the end of June 1943, Mrs. Zlatin sent a young non-Jewish girl from Montpellier, Renée Paillarès, to the Jewish vocational school at Laroche, near Agen in south-central France, to pick up Paul Niederman and Théo Reis and bring them to Izieu. Renée had gotten to know the boys in Hérault, and they had hit it off. Théo was also good friends with Renée's sister Paulette, who was spending the summer at Izieu as an assistant instructor.

In addition, Mrs. Zlatin had entrusted the girls' mother with Diane Popovski, a two-year-old whose parents, Symcha and Hélène, had been deported on September 11, 1942, and whom Mrs. Zlatin had personally sneaked out of Agde, hidden in a blanket. Diane spent part of the summer of 1943 at Izieu, then left with Paulette and her brother Guy for Montpellier. Her life saved by the Paillarès family, she lives today in Montreal.

When Paulette accepted Mrs. Zlatin's suggestion that she work as an instructor for the summer, she brought along not only Diane and her own father, but also her camera. It is thanks to this camera—and to Paulette herself, who kept the photos taken at Izieu—that the children of Izieu have not become faceless. In contrast, there is not a single photograph of any of the four thousand children arrested in the Paris raids of July 16 and 17, 1942, detained at the Vélodrome d'Hiver, and deported.

Paulette's photographs do not provide a picture of every child at the home. Some arrived at Izieu after that summer, and a number of those who appear in the group pictures left before the raid on April 6, 1944. A few crossed into Switzerland: Niederman, very tall and mature-looking for his sixteen years, caught the attention of the gendarmes upon his arrival in Belley and was subsequently entrusted to the EIF in Grenoble and helped across the border by OSE. Others were taken back by their parents: Bernard Waysenson and his brother were picked up by their father a few days before the raid and brought to a village in the department of Gard. The father, arrested shortly thereafter, was deported on May 15, 1944, in the same convoy as Mr. Zlatin, Reis, and Arnold Hirsch. Still others set out from Izieu in various directions and survived: Claude Reisz lives today in Perpignan; Alec Bergman, the best friend of Marcel Bulka, lives in Liège; and Yvette Benguigui, who at two years old was too young to stay at Izieu, also escaped the fate that gripped her three brothers.

Another survivor was Henry Alexander, who left France for the United States in 1947, and, after four years in Kansas City, settled in New York. Born March 28, 1927, at Neustadt in the Rhineland, Alexander arrived in France on March 8, 1939, with a group of child evacuees and was sheltered briefly at an OSE home outside Paris. He spent the next four years in a variety of institutions, seeing his parents for the last time in April 1941 within the camp perimeter at Gurs, where they were interned between their forced departure from Germany in October 1940 and their deportation from Drancy on August 10, 1942. In April 1943, when French gendarmes warned that the Jewish home in which he was staying might become the target of a German raid, Alexander was supplied with false papers and sent first to Chambéry, then on to the children's home at Izieu, which was just coming into existence.

Alexander remained at Izieu until September. "The atmosphere was quite agreeable," he recalls. "Théo Reis and I shared an attic room with a mattress on the floor. We used to listen to the radio, and when we heard about the bombing of Hamburg, we jumped for joy." During his months at the home, Alexander frequently traveled between Izieu and Chambéry carrying concealed documents; "I could go anywhere because I was still in short pants," he says, but adds that he was detained twice by the authorities, although released each time.

After leaving Izieu, Alexander made three unsuccessful attempts to cross the border into Switzerland. He was then taken under the wing of the EIF, supplied with false papers, given a fictitious Alsatian origin to account for his German accent, and slipped into the Compagnons de France, a paramilitary youth organization sponsored by Vichy. With the Compagnons and the EIF by turns, Alexander was involved in Resistance activity, and, before the war came to an end, was twice thrown into German prisons for interrogation.

Sabina Zlatin

The house from a distance.

The tension began to mount in September 1943, when the Germans moved into what had been the Italian-occupied zone. Before the end of the year, OSE had begun to wind down its legal activities, removing children from its homes, and placing them in hiding. Izieu, however, seemed a forgotten corner of the world, and life went on there much as before. Far from the cities where large Gestapo forces were likely to be concentrated, the home at Izieu also benefited from the cover furnished by the subprefecture at Belley and from the hospitality of the local population. In addition, the home was not an integral part of OSE. While that valiant organization contributed to the children's subsistence, it did so secretly—and therefore the existence and transfer of these funds did not figure at all on its books.

Nevertheless, danger was approaching. A Jewish doctor was arrested in the region; an OSE social worker, Margot Cohen, reported to Izieu and urged the dispersion of the children. Seeking out a more secure shelter for the group, Mrs. Zlatin left April 3 for a five-day trip to Montpellier. On April 5, Gabrielle Perrier, a twenty-one-year-old student-teacher assigned to the home since autumn through the kindness of the subprefecture in Belley, returned to her parents' home for Easter vacation. She would not be present during the raid on the following day.

The Raid

April 6 was a beautiful day. In the early morning, Léon Reifman got off the bus in Izieu. The subject of a search by the forced labor administration, he had left Izieu the previous September; his older sister, a doctor, had come to replace him as house medic, bringing along her parents and young son. Near the end of his journey from Montpellier, Léon had picked up Max Balsam and Marcel Mermelstein, boys from the Izieu home who had been placed in a boarding school near Belley and were returning for Easter vacation.

Toward nine in the morning, four vehicles drove up—two of them trucks—bearing soldiers and men in civilian dress. Coming on Maundy Thursday, the raid was a complete surprise. No one was standing watch, nor was there time to sound the alarm: the house bell, whose ring would have warned the children to scatter over the countryside. Only Léon Reifman—his sister calling, "Run for it!"—jumped, as if by reflex, out the window, and was lucky enough to escape.

All the others were taken: those who lived in the home itself; the two boys who had just arrived from Belley; and three others—Fritz Löbmann and the Goldberg brothers—who at this hour would have been at their jobs on local farms had it not been a holiday. One Lucien B., for whom Fritz worked under the name of François Loban, would later be suspected of having informed on the home.

Only one resident of the home was released: René Wucher, the only one of the children who was not a Jew. For it was against the Jews alone that the Gestapo's war was total. As our investigation has established, those children who were arrested and deported—all forty-four of them—were Jews.

In Montpellier, Mrs. Zlatin received a telegram from the subprefecture in Belley informing her of the raid. Marie-Antoinette Cojean had rushed to the scene, to find only the remnants of tragedy: unfinished bowls of hot chocolate testifying to a breakfast cut short. The children were packed off to Drancy the very next day; the speed with which Barbie's Gestapo effected their transfer precluded the attempts regional authorities would almost certainly have made to secure their release.

A resident of the village, a Mr. Vollet, recalls: "The day before, my son had brought them some Jerusalem artichokes. You saw the kids go by every day on their way to fetch the milk. We knew, of course, that they were taking away the Jews. But little children like that—that, we couldn't believe. By the time we found out, it was too late. Everyone in the village liked those little ones. We gave them apples; they were just kids."

According to the testimony of the villagers, Mr. Zlatin, who kept his wits about him, was beaten. The children were thrown "like packing cases" aboard the trucks. As they pulled away, these children—more than half of them of foreign origin—struck up a song they had learned from their French student-teacher: "Vous n'aurez pas l'Alsace et la Lorraine."

These were children whose parents had been arrested by the French police, acting upon Vichy's orders in the Free Zone, and handed over to the SS in the Occupied Zone. But they were also, and without a doubt, children who realized that the true France was to be found among their friends in Izieu, this tiny village where they had finally known some months of peace—leading the lives of normal children away at camp—before going to meet the terrible fate that awaited them where dawn breaks over Europe.

To Auschwitz

The testimony of Léa Feldblum, the only survivor of the raid and deportation, enables us to follow the route of the fifty-one prisoners. Jailed April 6 at Fort Montluc in Lyon, they were interrogated by turns before settling down for the night. The next day, under escort, the adults and older boys in manacles, they were transferred to Drancy in a passenger train. Then, as early as

34

On these and following pages: The children in
the summer of 1943, at and around the house
at Izieu. Top left: Guy Paillarès with little
Diane Popovski.

April 13, the first group from Izieu—thirty-four children, along with Léa and the Reifman family—was deported to Auschwitz.

The convoy that carried the majority of Izieu's residents was the seventy-first to leave France. Among its 1,500 deportees were 300 under the age of nineteen—almost half of these, 148, were under ten. There were many families in the convoy, including Barnett and Louise Greenberg with their nine children and Salomon and Clara Sephiha with their seven. Only ninety-one women and thirty-nine men from the seventy-first convoy survived deportation.

The train arrived at Auschwitz on the night of April 15, after a most painful voyage; on the platform at Birkenau, the selection took place. Although in possession of false papers, Léa had revealed her true identity at Drancy so that she could be deported with the children—her children. But when the officer in charge of the selection learned that the children were from a home, she was brutally separated from them. Little Emile Zuckerberg, an orphan who clung to Léa as if she were his mother, was ripped from her grasp. Léa was shoved toward the line of those whose murder was to be deferred—which allowed a small number, Léa among them, to survive, and to bear witness.

The thirty-four children and three other adults from Izieu were gassed that very day. The ten children and three adults still at Drancy were deported in later convoys.

None of them returned.

Barbie's Involvement

Even at the beginning of our attempt to bring Klaus Barbie to trial, we knew that we would never be able to establish with total certainty whether he himself was at Izieu. But we also felt—and our opinion has remained unchanged—that it is a question of minimal importance. For Barbie's crime consists in the fact that the authorization—or the order—to move against the children of

Right: Distribution of the mail at Izieu. Among the children are three adults: Miron Zlatin, director of the home (left); a medic, Léon Reifman, the only person to escape the raid (center); and the postman (right). Opposite: Among these children is Henry Alexander, top row center, who left Izieu before the raid. He settled in the United States after the war.

Izieu had to have come from him. This operation involved a foray some distance from Lyon; with partisans active in the area—Barbie himself headed a German column against them on the morning of April 8, at Larrivoire in the Jura—only the chief could have risked such a potentially dangerous operation. And Barbie's role is confirmed by the fact that he affixed his signature to the telex announcing the result of the raid at Izieu —a telex that would not have been signed by himself or by any of his subordinates in his name had responsibility for the raid not been entirely his.

Without the archives of the Lyon Gestapo, which were destroyed by the SS, exactly what happened can never be reconstructed. It is possible that Barbie, having learned of the home for Jewish children at Izieu through an informer, ordered one or more of his subordinates to go clear it out. It is equally possible that one of these subordinates had learned of the home's existence and requested authorization from his boss—Barbie—for the operation. Whatever the case, Barbie acted within his authority and of his own free will, with the result that these forty-four children were deported and killed. Barbie knew that arresting them and transferring them to Drancy spelled deportation; and, as a Gestapo officer with long experience in the organization, he could not have been unaware that, at such an advanced date as April 1944, deportation equaled death—especially for children between three and thirteen, like those he was adding to the balance sheet.

It is an absurd contention that Barbie's staff included specialists in Jewish affairs who took orders only from the anti-Jewish section of the Gestapo in Paris—or, better still, straight from Eichmann in Berlin. This well-known argument has been used and abused by the higher-ups of the Nazi police apparatus in France to no avail: Oberg and Knochen were tried and convicted in Paris in 1954; Lischka and Hagen were tried and convicted in Cologne in 1980. Eichmann did have a Paris representative —Röthke, head of the anti-Jewish section of the Gestapo in

France—and, beginning in June 1943, a special commando unit headed by Brunner that administered Drancy and directed special operations, such as the Nice roundups in the fall of 1943. However, anti-Jewish action on the part of regional Gestapo bureaus was essentially the responsibility of the regional commander and his subordinates.

Furthermore, Barbie's telex fails to include reference to any order from the anti-Jewish section in Paris regarding the home for Jewish children at Izieu. For all who are familiar with the meticulous bureaucracy of the Gestapo, this is the conclusive argument: it is hereby obvious that the liquidation of Izieu was strictly a local initiative on the part of the Gestapo at Lyon. Barbie was simply informing the anti-Jewish section of the Gestapo in Paris that the home at Izieu had been liquidated and that he would transfer the prisoners to Drancy the following day—Paris had not been aware of Izieu's existence, nor had it issued orders, as proven by the lack of reference to any previous communication whatever, be it letter, telex, memo, telegram, or telephone conversation. Moreover, if the operation had been carried out under the authority of any body other than the Lyon Gestapo, Barbie would inevitably have mentioned so in his message, like any Gestapo agent who is drawing up an accurate report—and it should be noted, that his telex, while brief, is precise.

Finally, appearing on previous telexes concerning Jewish matters are the abbreviations WE for Welti, and BA for Bartelmus (see documents on page 110). These two of Barbie's subordinates were more specifically in charge of Jewish matters for the Lyon bureau, although their criminality was many-sided. However, in the case of the Izieu telex—as in the case of two documents pertaining to the raid of the UGIF offices in Lyon on February 9, 1943—there are no initials of subordinates, except FI for Fiss, a telex operator in Lyon's Gestapo office.

The responsibility of the Lyon Gestapo in the affair of Izieu is total, as is the responsibility of its commander, Klaus Barbie.

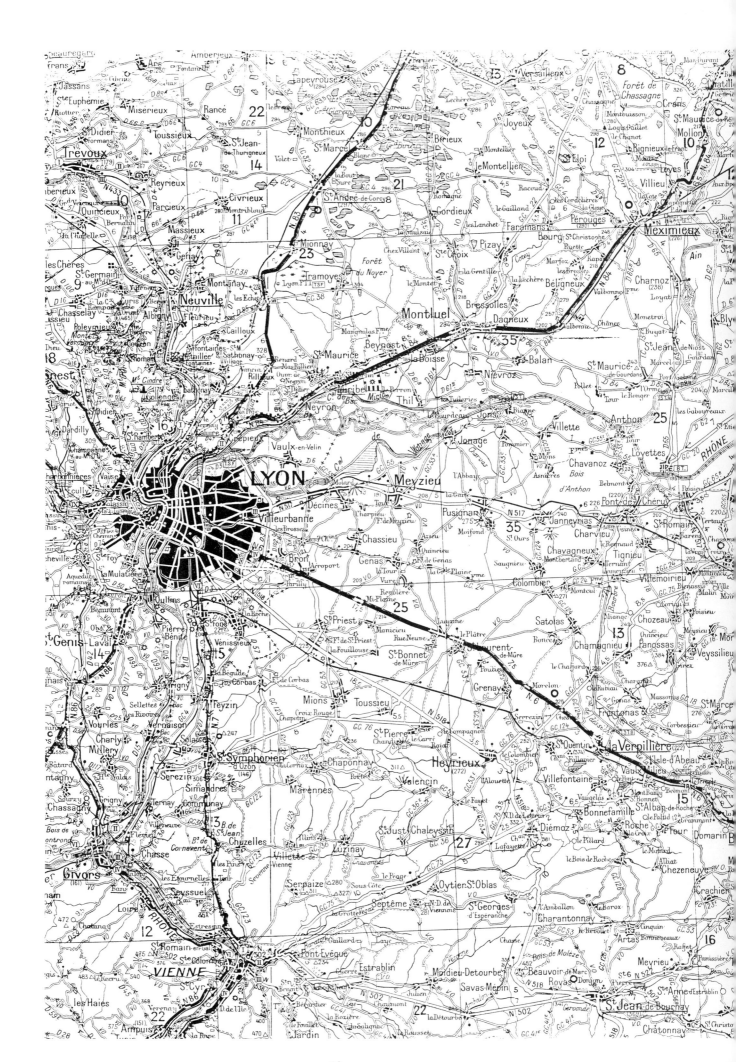

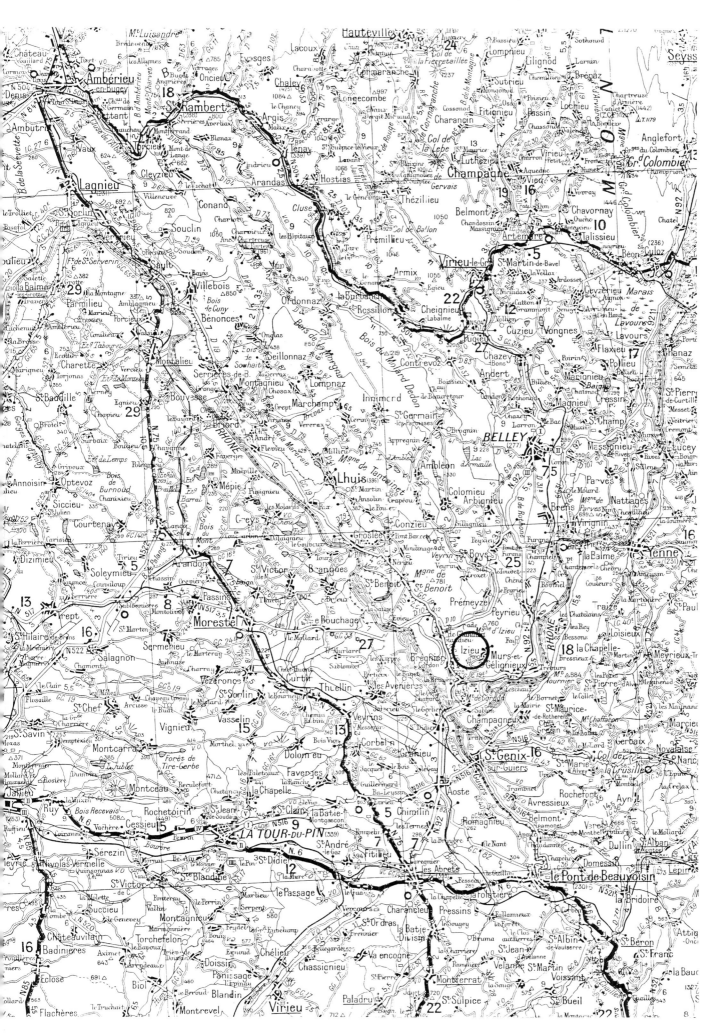

41

As this 1941 road map shows, the trip from
Lyon to Izieu (circled) was not a very long one.

THE CHILDREN

n Geburtsregister

register of births — Extracto del registro de nacimentos — Estratto del registro
en geboorte — Doğuma ait nüfus kayit hülâsasi su·eti — Izvod iz matične knjige
ĵenih.

Mannheim -/-	
30.10.1938 -/-	
M -/-	
Adelsheimer -/-	
Sami -/-	
-/-	
-/-	
Adelsheimer -/-	
Laura -/-	

Mannheim,

den 07.09.1983

Der Standesbeamte

Bernack We

Gebührenfrei

14 / 468

Sami Adelsheimer

· ·
Birth date: October 30, 1938   Birthplace: Mannheim, Germany
· ·

Sami's mother, Laura Adelsheimer, was born October 3, 1897, at Lemförde, Germany, one of three children of Louis and Pauline Adelsheimer. Deported in convoy number sixty-two, which left Drancy on November 20, 1943, she was murdered in Auschwitz.

Sami was deported in convoy number seventy-one. His cousin, Ruth Adelsheimer, lives in Israel and is an associate plaintiff in the Barbie case.

Birth certificate of Sami Adelsheimer.

Hans Ament

Birth date: February 15, 1934 • • • • • • • • • • • Birthplace: Vienna, Austria

Hans was the son of Max Ament, born June 28, 1895, in Sanok, Poland, and Ernestina Reisz Ament, born September 29, 1902, in Budapest. Having left Austria for Belgium in 1939, the family planned to emigrate to America. A U.S. visa was issued to Hans on March 22, 1940, in Antwerp, but before he was able to leave, the Germans invaded Belgium and his family was forced to flee instead to France.

Max Ament was deported on March 4, 1943, in convoy number fifty from Drancy, and was murdered at either Sobibor or Maidanek. On March 23, 1943, Ernestina Ament entered the sanatorium L'Espérance in Hauteville, several dozen kilometers from the home at Izieu, suffering from tuberculosis; she died on August 7, 1944.

Hans Ament was deported on May 30, 1944, in convoy number seventy-five. His brother Alfred, older by six years, was smuggled by OSE into Switzerland. He lives today in the United States, and is an associate plaintiff.

Above: Hans Ament (left).

Hans, who preferred to be called Jean, his name's French equivalent, was at Izieu when he sent this letter and drawing to his mother in the sanatorium. The German annotation in the upper right-hand corner—"I am sending you everything, keep it as a memento"—is a note to Hans's brother Alfred from the boys' aunt. The letter itself, signed "Jeannot," the diminutive of Jean, is in somewhat flawed French:

Dear Mommy,

Thanks for your letter, I was happy to get it. I haven't written you because I didn't have any paper, but a boy gave me some. It's hardly snowing here anymore. Are you almost better, and if you're all right over there. I'm eating well, and I'm in good health. Is it cold where you are and write me if it's snowing. When there was a lot of snow here we went tobogganing on the slopes. We had a real good time. Write Freddy that he shouldn't write me in German. There's a nice dog at the home we call Sami. The school is in the house and there's a special teacher for school. She does a good job teaching us. Next to the house there's a farm with four dogs. 100,000,000 big kisses from your son Jeannot who is always thinking of you.

Jeannot

See over

Nina Aronowicz

. . . .

Birth date: November 28, 1932   Birthplace: Brussels, Belgium

. . . .

Nina was the daughter of Szyje-Leib Aronowicz, born February 24, 1902, in Kozmink, Poland, and Mieckla Seiler Aronowicz, born October 14, 1903, in Kalisz, Poland.

The Aronowicz family had plans to emigrate to the United States. At the end of 1941, Nina wrote to her uncle and aunt, who had succeeded in crossing the Atlantic: "We are very happy that you are already in America. We wish we were there already. Do you like America?" However, as refugees at Palavas-les-Flots, Nina's parents realized they were soon to be arrested by the Vichy police, and they entrusted their daughter to the Regnats, a non-Jewish family who took the child into their home in Lunel, some twenty miles northeast of Montpellier.

In a letter dated September 18, 1944, Mr. Regnat wrote:

A few days later, the mother was arrested and taken to a camp near Perpignan. We received word from her from the camp at Drancy, and then nothing. As for the father, who had managed to elude the police, we last heard over a year ago from the Saint-Louis Hospital in Perpignan. We kept Nina with us for about eight months after the Germans invaded the Free Zone, but then we had to hand her over to Mrs. Slaten [sic], a social worker from Montpellier. This took place in the spring of 1943, and the last news we had came from the children's home in Izieu, Ain, ten months ago.

Nina's mother had been deported September 11, 1942, in convoy number thirty-one, and murdered in Auschwitz. Nina's father had met the same fate after having been deported December 7, 1943, in convoy number sixty-four. After leaving the Regnats, Nina stayed a short time in the Jewish children's home at Campestre, from which she was transferred with other children to Izieu.

On July 3, 1943, Nina wrote from Izieu to her Aunt Constance in Paris:

I am very happy to be here. There are beautiful mountains, and from high up you can see the Rhone flow by, and it's very pretty. Yesterday we went for a swim in the Rhone with Miss Marcelle (that's a teacher). Sunday we had a birthday party for Paulette and two other children and we put on a lot of skits and it was really great. And July 25 we're going to have another party in honor of the house.

Nina Aronowicz was deported in convoy number seventy-one. Her paternal uncle lives in Israel and is an associate plaintiff on her behalf, as is the widow of her maternal uncle.

Nina Aronowicz—who went by the name "Mina"—wrote this letter to her Aunt Constance on February 9, 1944:

My dear Auntie,

This morning I got your nice letter and your money order. I was very glad to get them. Thank you very much.

I am feeling well and I hope you, Mimi, and Jacky are, too. I'm still going to school. Does Jacky go? I imagine he does.

It's snowing here, and the boys are making a snowman. Don't bother sending me a package, because I have plenty to eat and don't need anything. I got a package with books from Mr. R. for Christmas. For Mardi Gras, we're going to throw a party and have a real good time. I'm fine here and I'm eating well.

I hope to see you again soon, and while awaiting this pleasure I say good-bye, hugging you as hard as I can, and also Mimi and Jacques.

Mina

Below: Birth certificate of Nina Aronowicz.
Bottom: Nina with members of her family, including her parents (to Nina's right and slightly behind her).

Ville de Bruxelles.
2ᵉ DISTRICT

Stad Brussel.
2ᵉ DISTRICT

Nº 675 ____ L'an mil neuf cent trente-deux, le trente novembre, à neuf heures du matin, _____
Het jaar duizend negenhonderd

Nom: Jules COELST, _____ officier de l'état civil de la Ville de Bruxelles 2ᵉ district, dressons l'acte de naissance
De ambtenaar van den Burgerlijken Stand der Stad Brussel 2ᵉ district de geboorteakte op

de Nina, née le vingt-huit de ce mois, à cinq heures du matin, Place Van Gehuchten, Nº 4, 8e division; fille de Bays
Leib A R O N O W I C Z, opticien, âgé de trente ans, né à Kozminek (Kalish Russie), et de Michla Seiler, sans profession, âgée de vingt-neuf ans, née à Kalisz, (Koleh Russie), conjointe résidant à Schaerbeek, rue Lefrancq, Nº 19, et
domiciliés à Kaltes (Kalish Pologne).- Sur la déclaration de Charles Housquin, directeur de l'hôpital Brugmann, âgé
cinquante-six ans, domicilié à Bruxelles deuxième district.- En présence de Guillaume Govaerts, messager, âgé de qua-
deux ans, domicilié à Grimberghen, et de Jacques Moermans, messager, âgé de trente-neuf ans, domicilié à Jette.- Ap
lecture, Nous avons signé avec le déclarant et les témoins.- Kalish; Kalisz renvois approuvé ainsi que la rature d
deux mots.

VILLE DE BRUXELLES - STAD BRUSSEL
2ᵉ District - 2de District

Pour copie conforme - Voor eensluitend afschrift

Bruxelles II, le
Brussel II,   21. V. 1984

Pour l'Officier de l'état civil.

Max-Marcel Balsam

. . . .

Birth date: May 15, 1931   Birthplace: Paris, France

. . . .

Jean-Paul Balsam

. . . .

Birth date: June 6, 1933   Birthplace: Paris, France

. . . .

The boys' father, Salomon Balsam, was born December 7, 1893, in Warsaw; he was deported in the first convoy to leave France, on March 27, 1942, and was murdered in Auschwitz on April 24, 1942. Their mother, Selma Halberg Balsam, was originally from Germany. The couple also had two daughters, Hélène and Berthe. The family lived in Paris.

After Selma Balsam had left with Berthe for the Lyon suburb of Villeurbanne, where they took up residence on rue Henri-Rolland, the other three children and their grandmother, Tauba Halberg (born in 1873 in Bugzacz, Poland), were arrested during the big roundup of February 1943. The grandmother was deported in convoy number forty-nine on March 2, 1943.

The three children were released from Drancy, and, after transfer to the UGIF children's center in the rue Vauquelin in Paris, they were reunited with their mother in Villeurbanne. Jean-Paul was then placed at Izieu, and Max at the Catholic boarding school in nearby Belley.

At Easter vacation, Max went to visit Jean-Paul; Léon Reifman picked him up at the school early on the morning of April 6, 1944, and brought him by bus to Izieu. Max and Jean-Paul were deported in convoy number seventy-one.

Their two sisters had been unaware of the tragedy, and it was three days after the raid, when their turn came to visit their brothers at Izieu, that they learned what had happened.

The three survivors emigrated to Brazil. Hélène, the only one alive today, is an associate plaintiff.

- BALSAM, Hélène	16.I.1929 Paris Française	73, rue Charlot, Paris
- BALSAM Jean-Paul	6.6.1933 Paris Française	73,rue Charlé Paris
- BALSAM,Max, Marcel	15.5.1931 Paris Française	73, rue Charlot Paris

SORTIES-LIBERATIONS

BALSAM Hélène	16.I.29 Paris Franç.	p des A.A. pour être confié à l'U.G.I.F.
BALSAM Jean-Paul Fr.	6.6.33 Paris	do
BALSAM Marx Marcel FR.	15.5.31 Paris	do

Top: Max above, Jean-Paul below. Upper document: Excerpt from the list of those arrested in the raid of February 15, 1943, in Paris. Indicated are birth date, nationality, and address. Lower document: Excerpt from the list of "Departures-Releases" from Drancy on March 30, 1943. Indicated are nationality, birth date, city of residence, and circumstances of release: "by decision of the German Authorities [A.A.; Authorités Allemandes], to be placed in custody of UGIF." Left: Jean-Paul left, Max right.

Esther Benassayag

. . . .
Birth date: April 29, 1931   Birthplace: Region of Oran, Algeria
. . . .

Elie Benassayag

. . . .
Birth date: November 20, 1933   Birthplace: Region of Oran, Algeria
. . . .

Jacob Benassayag

. . . .
Birth date: September 1, 1935   Birthplace: Region of Oran, Algeria
. . . .

There were six children in the Benassayag family. Their father, David Benassayag, born May 14, 1901, in Reibell, Algeria, became a policeman after the family had moved to Marseilles. Their mother, Fortunée Partouche Benassayag, was born in Mostaganem, Algeria, on July 14, 1903.

David Benassayag was arrested on January 23, 1943, during the mass roundup in Marseilles and deported on March 23, 1943, to Sobibor, where he was murdered.

Esther, Elie, and Jacob, the three children entrusted to the home at Izieu, were deported in convoy number seventy-one. One of their brothers is an associate plaintiff.

Il reste toutefois à noter que la plupart des familles n'ayant pas quitté Marseille ont vu leurschefs arrêtés en Janvier dernier et sont demeurées avec de nombreux enfants, ce qui expliquerait également un budget important pour un plus petit nombre de cas.

Nous nous devons d'attirer l'attention sur le fait que/les familles nombreuses composant la majorité de nos cas, il deviendrai de plus en plus nécessaire de créer un service social organisé. Malheureusement, nous ne voyons que trop l'impossibilité dans

---

Excerpt of a report by the social welfare department of the UGIF Marseilles bureau. The report, dated April 1, 1943, outlines the situation of families like the Benassayags:

Nonetheless, it remains to be noted that most of the families that did not leave Marseilles saw the heads of their households arrested last January. That families with many children have stayed on would also explain the high budget for a smaller case load.

We must also draw attention to the fact that, as large families make up the majority of our cases, setting up organized social services would become more and more necessary. Unfortunately, the impossibility of this is only too clear to us in...

Top: Esther Benassayag (arrow) in the yard of
an elementary school in Marseilles. Above:
Elie and Jacob Benassayag (arrows) in the
same schoolyard.

Jacques Benguigui

Birth date: April 13, 1931 · · · · · · · · · · · Birthplace: Oran, Algeria

Richard Benguigui

Birth date: March 31, 1937 · · · · · · · · · · · Birthplace: Oran, Algeria

Jean-Claude Benguigui

Birth date: December 26, 1938 · · · · · · · · · · · Birthplace: Oran, Algeria

The boys' mother, Fortunée Chouraki Messaouda, was born April 30, 1904, in Oran, Algeria. Arrested in Marseilles, she was deported to Auschwitz on July 31, 1943, in convoy number fifty-eight, and subjected to medical experiments in the camp's infamous Block 10. It was there that she learned of the deportation and murder of her three boys. By the time she was liberated, her weight had fallen to around eighty pounds. Despite her poor health, she provided a great lesson in compassion: immediately following her liberation from Auschwitz, she took care for a time of a paralyzed German woman who was the mother of two children.

All that remained to Mrs. Benguigui upon her return to France were the aftermath of her suffering and her little daughter, Yvette, born March 2, 1941, who had been too young to stay at the home in Izieu and had been entrusted to farmers in the area. The battle Mrs. Benguigui waged at the side of Beate Klarsfeld is recounted in the chapter, "Two Mothers of Izieu Struggle to Bring Barbie to Justice."

Jacques Benguigui drew remarkably well for his age. The following letter, which he wrote to his mother on May 30, 1943, brings tears to our eyes each time we read it, so clear is the mark of an exceptional nature:

O Mother,

My dear Mother, I know how greatly you have suffered for me and, on this joyous Mother's Day, I send you from afar the loving wishes that fill my little child's heart. Though far from you, I have done, darling Mother, all I could to make you happy: when you send me packages, I share them with those who no longer have parents. Mother, my dear Mother, I say good-bye with hugs and kisses.

Your son, who loves you dearly.

The three boys were deported in convoy number seventy-one, which left Drancy on April 13, 1944—Jacques's thirteenth birthday. Mrs. Benguigui and her daughter, Yvette, are associate plaintiffs.

Opposite: Letter from twelve-year-old Jacques Benguigui to his grandparents in Algeria, dated November 9, 1943. Jacques has apparently substituted the term "communion" for Bar Mitzvah. His rather unorthodox notion of French spelling is not reflected in the English translation:

Tuesday, November 9

Dear Grandparents,

I was very glad to get your letter. You tell me that I'll be coming to Algeria for my communion. When I saw that, I jumped for joy. I hope that you are in good health, because you don't have to worry about me because I put on six pounds in a month and I continue to eat well. You say you're going to send me a package, and I was very happy to have read that. I'd like you to send me oranges and tangerines if there are any. If this letter is poorly written it's because I don't have any time. If I had the time I would have written you four pages. It's going to snow soon. We're going to go tobogganing. And now to make the letter longer I send you a hug. Millions of good wishes for everybody.

Jacques

Above, left to right: Jean-Claude, Richard, and Jacques Benguigui. Above right: Drawing by Jacques Benguigui for Mother's Day, May 1943. Inscriptions read "Long Live Mommy" and "Happy Mother's Day." Right: Excerpt from the roster for convoy number seventy-one, which left Drancy for Auschwitz on Jacques Benguigui's thirteenth birthday. The boys' birth dates are all incorrectly listed; Jacques and Richard are listed as school-children, Jean-Claude as without occupation.

77	BENGUIGUI	Jacques	10. 4.31	Schüler	19XO2
78	BENGUIGUI	Jean Claude	32	Ohne	19I2e
79	BENGUIGUI	Richard	29. 3.37	Schüler	I9I22

51

Barouk-Raoul Bentitou

. . . .
Birth date: May 27, 1931   Birthplace: Palikao, Algeria
. . . .

Of this family of eight children, the father and three brothers were murdered by the Nazis. Abraham Bentitou, born October 21, 1900, in Palikao, was arrested during the mass roundup in Marseilles on January 23, 1943, with two of his sons, Maurice, born March 24, 1922, in Palikao, and André, born October 28, 1923, in Palikao. All three were deported to Sobibor on March 23, 1943.

According to the account of Paulette Paillarès, Barouk-Raoul sang all the time. He was deported in convoy number seventy-one. His brother is an associate plaintiff.

Barouk-Raoul Bentitou, second from left, in a photograph taken at Izieu during the summer of 1943.

52

Majer (Marcel) Bulka

Birth date: September 29, 1930   Birthplace: Kalisz, Poland

Albert Bulka

Birth date: June 28, 1939   Birthplace: Ougrée, Belgium

The Bulka family was interned at Rivesaltes, but the children were taken from the camp and placed at the home at Palavas-les-Flots. Their mother, Roizel Moskowicz Bulka, born August 18, 1903, in Warda, Poland, was transferred from Rivesaltes to Drancy and deported in convoy number thirty-one on September 11, 1942; she was murdered in Auschwitz. Their father, Mosiek-Chaïm Bulka, born June 4, 1901, in Boleslawice, Poland, was transferred from Rivesaltes to Gurs on February 26, 1943. He was sent to Drancy on March 2, 1943, and deported two days later in convoy number fifty to either Maidanek or Sobibor, where he was murdered.

The two brothers were deported in convoy number seventy-one. The boys' maternal uncle, who lives in the United States, is an associate plaintiff.

Top: Marcel (left) and Albert Bulka (center) with Alec Bergman, Marcel's best friend, who left Izieu before the raid. The photograph was taken on the terrace at Izieu. Above: Little Marcel Bulka, foreground center, in a photograph of the Bulka and Moskowicz families taken in Poland. Left: Marcel Bulka with his parents. From left to right: Convoy number thirty-one, murdered 1942; convoy number seventy-one, murdered 1944; convoy number fifty, murdered 1943.

53

Lucienne Friedler

Birth date: February 18, 1939   **Birthplace: Berchem (Antwerp), Belgium**

Lucienne was an only child. She had fled Belgium with her parents at the beginning of May 1940, during the German invasion; the family was interned in the Free Zone. Her mother, Mina Kunstler Friedler, born February 20, 1912, in Turku, Poland, was a member of the staff at Izieu. Both she and her daughter were deported in convoy number seventy-six on June 30, 1944.

Lucienne's father, Isidoor, born May 14, 1915, at The Hague, Netherlands, was deported to Auschwitz by individual transport from Compiègne, in the North Zone, during the summer of 1943. Ultimately liberated at Gusen, a sub-camp of Mauthausen in Austria, he lives today in Israel; he is an associate plaintiff. His own parents were killed during an attempt to slip across the Swiss border.

Birth certificate of Lucienne Friedler. Her face remains a blank, as not even her father has a photograph of her.

INTERNATIONALE OVEREENKOMST AFGIFTE VAN AKTEN VAN DE BURGERLIJKE STAND
(Wet van 18 juli 1974 - Belg. Stbl. 31 december 1974)

Uittreksel uit geboorteakte

1939/107   A

a plaats van geboorte lieu de naissance Geburtsort place of birth lugar de nacimiento luogo di nascita dogum yeri	Berchem thans Antwerpen district Berchem	f familienaam van de vader nom de famille du père Familienname des Vaters surname of the father apellido del padre cognome del padre babasinin soyadi	Friedler
b datum van geboorte date de naissance Geburtsdatum date of birth fecha de nacimiento data di nascita dogum tarihi	18.02.1939	g voornamen van de vader prénoms du père Vornamen des Vaters christian names of the father nombres de pila del padre prenomi del padre babasinin adi	Isidoor
c geslacht van het kind sexe de l'enfant Geschlecht des Kindes sex of the child sexo del niño sesso del bambino çocugun cinsiyeti	f.	h meisjesnaam van de moeder nom de jeune fille de la mère Madchenname der Mutter maiden name of the mother apellido de soltera de la madre nome di signorina della madre anasinin evlenmeden önceki soyadi	Kunstler
d familienaam van het kind nom de famille de l'enfant Familienname des Kindes surname of the child apellido del niño cognome del bambino çocugun soyadi	Friedler	i voornamen van de moeder prénoms de la mère Vornamen der Mutter christian names of the mother nombres de pila de la madre prenomi della madre anasinin adi	Mina
e voornamen van het kind prénoms de l'enfant Vornamen des Kindes christian names of the child nombres de pila del niño prenomi del bambino çocugun adi	Lucienne		

2 1 MEI 1984

datum van afgifte. ondertekening en zegel van de bewaarder.
date de délivrance. signature et sceau du dépositaire.
Ausstellungsdatum. Unterschrift und Dienstsiegel des Registerführers.
date of issue. signature and seal of keeper.
fecha de expedición. firma y sello del depositario.
data in cui è stato rilasciato l'atto, con firma e bollo dell' ufficio.
verildigi tarih nufus (ahvali sahsiye) memurunun imzasi ve mührü

Voor de Ambtenaar van de Burgerlijke Stand,
De gemachtigde beambte

Laurent Jean

Egon-Heinrich Gamiel

. . . .
Birth date: May 18, 1934   Birthplace: Argenschwang, Germany
. . . .

Egon's parents, Ernest Gamiel, born October 15, 1904, in Argenschwang, and Gertrude Harf Gamiel, born March 19, 1904, in Seibersbach, Germany, were interned at Les Milles, then turned over by Vichy to the Nazis. They were deported in convoy number twenty on August 17, 1942. In the same convoy were Gertrude's sister, Ida Harf Hirsch, and her husband, Max, the parents of Egon's cousin Arnold Hirsch, who was also at Izieu. Both couples were murdered at Auschwitz.

Egon, an only child, was deported in convoy number seventy-one. Doris Harf, the first cousin of Ida and Gertrude, lives in the United States and is associate plaintiff on behalf of Egon Gamiel and Arnold Hirsch, her first cousins once removed.

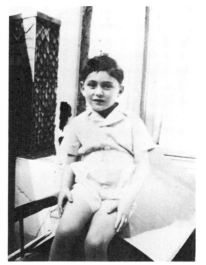

Listed on the same page of the roster for car number two in convoy number twenty (left), which left Drancy August 17, 1942, are the parents of Egon Gamiel and Arnold Hirsch, first cousins who were together at Izieu. Max Hirsch (number 26) and Ida Harf Hirsch (28) are listed as *agriculteur* and *agricultrice*, farmers; Ernst Gamiel (37) is listed as *cultivateur*, also a farmer; Gertrude Harf Gamiel (39), Ida's sister, is listed as *sp*, for *sans profession*, without profession.

```
                        WAGON N° 2

25 -HUNBERT Lola           14.10.07 Ostrau    Ex-Autrich.     Modiste
     née IMERGLUECK

26-HIRSCH Max              8.10.98 Argensthwang  All.          Agriculteur

27-HOVEL Melitra           14.4.86 Altdorf        "            sp

28-HIRSCH Ida              3.12.00 Seiberbach      "            Agricultrice
     née HARF

29-HIRSCH Eugène Fritz     8.4.97 Hambourg         "            Ingénieur

30-HIRSCH Löbel            24.2.93 Cracovie    Ex-Autrich.     Libraire

31 HIRSCH Martin           3.3.89 Polszin      All.            Commerçant

32-HESS Wilhem             27.10.92 Neuerburg     "             "

33-HAHAN Léopold           24.9.02 Vienne      Ex-Autrich.     Maroquinier

34-HEYMANN Walter          17.12.23 Hof         All.           Jardinier

35-HUNDERT Joseph          7.8.83 Obertyn      Ex-Autrich.     Commerçant

36-BLATT Heinz             9.3.10 Berlin       All.            Professeur
                                                               d'éd.physique

37-GAMIEL Ernst            15.10.04 Argenschwaing  "           Cultivateur

38-BLATT Elly              27.1.04 Berlin          "           sp
     née KOHN

39-GAMIEL Gertrude NéeHARF 19.3.04 Seibersbach     "           sp

40-HAAS Georges            21.4.95 Vienne      Ex-Autrich.     Orfèvre

41 GOTTLIEB Michel         27.11.97 Vienne         "           Représentant

42-HAAS Robert             18.2.00 Vienne          "           Fonctionnaire

43-HERZ Hilde              6.9.98 Adelsberg     All.           sp

44-HIRSCH Emily Née HESS   23.2.00 Lubeck       Réf. All.      sp

45-HERZ Léon               10.4.97 Gémund       All.           Commerçant

46-HESS Nani Née LAZARUS   8.9.95 Treves           "           Couturière

47-HIRSCH Alfred           7.7.89 Augfzburg        "           Commerçant
48-HUNDERT Hermann         25.8.09 Horbenka    Ex-Autrich.     Agriculteur
49-HOBEL Isaac             6.9.87 Urspiringen   All.           Professeur
50-HUPPERT Charles         12.6.92 Vienne      Ex-Autrich.     Expert-Comptable
51-GOTTLIEB Gertrude       6.7.01 Vienne           "           Employée
     née HAAS
```

Maurice Gerenstein

Birth date: January 3, 1931   Birthplace: Paris, France

Liliane Gerenstein

Birth date: January 13, 1933   Birthplace: Nice, France

The parents of Maurice and Liliane, Chapse Alexandre Gerenstein, born August 23, 1901, in Odessa, Russia, and Chendla Entine Gerenstein, born January 10, 1903, in Odessa, were both deported on November 20, 1943, in convoy number sixty-two, to Auschwitz, where Mrs. Gerenstein was murdered. Mr. Gerenstein, a musician, played trumpet in the camp orchestra at Auschwitz; he survived and emigrated to the United States.

Liliane wrote a heart-rending letter, addressed to God, only days before her arrest. The letter was found at Izieu after the raid.

God? How good You are, and how kind, and if we had to count all You have bestowed upon us that is good and kind, our counting would be without end.... God? It is You who command. It is You who are justice. It is You who reward the good and punish the evil. God? I can therefore say that I will never forsake You. I will always be mindful of You, even to the last moments of my life. You can be absolutely certain of that. For me, You are something beyond words, so good are You. You may believe me. God? It is thanks to You that I enjoyed a wonderful life before, that I was spoiled, that I had lovely things, things that others do not have. God? As a result, I ask just one thing of You: BRING BACK MY PARENTS, MY POOR PARENTS, PROTECT THEM (even more than myself) SO THAT I MAY SEE THEM AS SOON AS POSSIBLE. HAVE THEM COME BACK ONE MORE TIME. Oh! I can say that I have had such a good mother, and such a good father! I have such faith in You that I thank You in advance.

Maurice, along with Max Balsam, was brought back to Izieu by Léon Reifman on the morning of the raid; the boarding school that the two boys were attending in nearby Belley had recessed for Easter.

Both Maurice and Liliane were deported in convoy number seventy-one. A cousin living in the United States is associate plaintiff on their behalf.

Liliane Gerenstein's letter to God, praying for the safety of her parents.

Le trois janvier mil neuf cent trente-un, six heures, est né, Cité des Fleurs,
9, Maurice, du sexe masculin, de Chapse GERENSTEIN, né à Odessa (Russie) le
vingt-trois août mil neuf cent un, musicien, et de Schendla ENTINE, née à Odessa (Russie) le dix janvier mil neuf cent trois, sans profession, son épouse,
domiciliés rue Ramey, 38. Dressé le six janvier mil neuf cent trente-un, dix
heures, sur la déclaration du père, qui, lecture faite a signé avec Nous, Jean
Edouard Michel SCHWENCK, adjoint au Maire du dix,septième arrondissement de
Paris./:

Vu C.A. le 13-1-43

N° 149
Gerenstein
Liliane

Le treize janvier _____ mil neuf cent trente-trois
neuf heures
est née rue du Congrès, 13
Liliane
du sexe féminin
de Chapse Gerenstein,
musicien, né à Odessa (Russie) le
vingt trois août mil neuf cent un et de
Chendla Entine, son épouse
sans profession, née à Odessa, le
premier Octobre mil neuf cent trois
domiciliés à Nice

Dressé le seize janvier _____ mil neuf cent trente-trois
quatorze heures, sur la déclaration du père

qui, lecture faite _____ a signé avec Nous Jean GRINETTA

Conseiller Municipal de la Ville de Nice, Officier de l'Etat-Civil par
délégation

Gerenstein

Birth certificates of Maurice (top) and Liliane Gerenstein.

Henri-Chaïm Goldberg

Birth date: December 30, 1930   Birthplace: Paris, France

Joseph Goldberg

Birth date: March 1, 1932   Birthplace: Paris, France

Henri and Joseph were the children of Gita and Amyl Goldberg. While at Izieu, they sometimes worked on the nearby farm of a Mr. Perticoz. Joseph, who sent drawings to his mother, wrote to her:

> You tell me that I am a fine artist as far as drawings go, but that I am not yet a painter; later, perhaps, that depends. As soon as we got your letter, we read it, and we took it to the director. She read it, and then gave us a little lecture, which I enjoyed. She told us that we had to study hard, because if we didn't, when you saw us again after the war, we'd be dunces. So I am going to study hard in order to please you, in order to please the director and the teacher, and in order to please myself, too. That way, after the war you'll see that we're both intelligent, and you won't look at us like dummies.

The two boys were deported in convoy number seventy-one. Their half-brother is an associate plaintiff.

Above: Drawing by Joseph Goldberg, inscribed: "For my darling mother, whom I am sending this drawing. Your son, Joseph." Right: Excerpt from Joseph Goldberg's letter to his mother.

Henri and Joseph Goldberg, second and third
from left. At far left is a local farmer.

Mina Halaunbrenner

Birth date: June 25, 1935   Birthplace: Paris, France

Claudine Halaunbrenner

Birth date: April 2, 1939   Birthplace: Paris, France

Excerpted deposition of Alexandre Halaunbrenner (born October 28, 1931, in Paris), taken by the Klarsfelds and submitted to the Munich prosecutor's office in 1971:

From 1941 to 1943, [our family was] interned in several camps in the South Zone (Nexon, Rivesaltes, Gurs). On August 26, 1943, we were placed in assigned residence in Lyon.

We were living at 14 Rue Pierre-Loti in Villeurbanne when the Gestapo came to our house at 11:00 A.M. on October 24, 1943. There were three men. Two were tall and about forty years old; the third, who was younger—to my childish eyes, he seemed about thirty—was plainly in command. He waited impatiently on the chance that my father's nephew —who must have been denounced to the Gestapo, which arrested and killed him in 1944—might arrive. While my sisters clung to my father, the younger man drew his revolver, terrifying us. His face has been etched in my memory ever since this moment, which has haunted my dreams and my sleepless nights. When I saw a photograph published in Die Weltwoche on September 10, 1971, I recognized him at once, as did my mother, who was there beside me.

My brother Léon, who was very tall for his age, came home about 6:00 P.M. The three Gestapo men had been at our apartment continuously until then, one of them standing watch outside the door. When my brother arrived, they searched him, then decided to take him away, along with my father. My mother began to shout in Yiddish for them to let my brother go, and we all wept and screamed, but in vain. Barbie shoved my mother aside as she tried to keep them from leaving; he drew his revolver again and struck her hand to make her let go.

It was all to no avail. We spent the night in the street, my little sisters clinging to my mother's skirts as she watched for the return of the two arrestees. It was when we saw a German army truck stop in front of our house—undoubtedly to take us away in our turn—that, pretending to be passers-by, we walked away, leaving everything behind.

A few weeks later, on December 14, we learned from a Jewish friend that my father had died "in the hospital." My mother and I immediately went through all the hospitals, without turning up anything. It then occurred to me to go to the morgue. "He's been here three weeks," the attendant told us. He had been shot in a summary execution at the Ecole de Santé on Rue Marcelin-Barthelot, headquarters of the Gestapo. Seventeen machine-gun bullets were in his neck and chest.

My brother Léon was deported and worked to total exhaustion in the Polish salt mines. He died in eight months.

Two of my sisters, Mina and Claudine, were placed by UGIF and OSE in the home for Jewish children at Izieu. We believed that they were safe. Tragically, Barbie did not spare them; he liquidated the children's home on April 6, 1944. My sisters were deported on June 30, 1944, and were murdered upon arrival at Auschwitz.

Mina and Claudine were the daughters of Jacob Halaunbrenner, born July 12, 1902, in Drogobycz, Austria (now Poland), and Ita-Rosa Hoffner Halaunbrenner, born August 7, 1904, in Fustonowicz, Poland. The Halaunbrenners had five children. The eldest was Léon, born April 21, 1929, in Drogobycz; the Lyon Gestapo arrested him along with his father on October 24, 1943. Léon was transferred to Drancy and deported December 17, 1943, in convoy number sixty-three to Auschwitz; his father was imprisoned in Fort Montluc before being executed by Barbie's men on November 24, 1943.

Mrs. Halaunbrenner reluctantly decided to part with Mina and Claudine, whom OSE sent by way of its underground network to Izieu. The two girls were deported to Auschwitz in convoy number seventy-six on June 30, 1944, two-and-a-half months after most of their fellows from the children's home.

Alexandre, born October 28, 1931, and Monique, born December 5, 1941, both in Paris, stayed with their mother; all three survived the war, and fervently cherish the memory of the four members of their family who fell victim to the anti-Jewish racism of the Nazis. Mrs. Halaunbrenner's justly renowned exploits at the side of Beate Klarsfeld in Bolivia in 1972 are described in the chapter entitled "Two Mothers of Izieu Struggle to Bring Barbie to Justice."

Above: The Halaunbrenners, a family almost totally wiped out by the Lyon Gestapo. Left to right: Jacob, the father, executed in Lyon; Claudine, deported from Izieu; the three survivors, Ita-Rosa, the mother, Monique, in her arms, and Alexandre; Mina, deported from Izieu; and Léon, deported from Lyon. Left: Mrs. Halaunbrenner received official notice of her husband's death at the hands of the Germans in a letter from the prefecture of the department of Rhône dated March 21, 1959:

Madame,

In response to your letter of February 27, 1959, I have the honor of certifying to you that, according to the information included in his alien's file, your husband, Halaundrenner [sic], Jacob, born July 12, 1902, in Drohobrycy [sic], Poland, was interned at Fort de Montluc in Lyon in October 1943 and shot dead by the Germans at the Ecole de Santé Militaire on November 24, 1943. Death certificate no. 1049, issued by the main administrative offices for the seventh arrondissement.

I authorize you to make use of this letter for administrative purposes.

Sincerely,

For the Prefect of the Rhône:
The Deputy Chief of Staff

FM/GP

PRÉFECTURE

DU RHÔNE

RÉPUBLIQUE FRANÇAISE
LIBERTÉ · ÉGALITÉ · FRATERNITÉ

LYON, le 21 MAR 1959

1 DIVISION
BUREAU
3

DR : 86 404 CG.

Madame,

     En réponse à votre lettre du 27 février 1959, j'ai l'honneur de vous confirmer que suivant les indications figurant à son dossier d'étranger, votre mari HALAUNDRENNER Jacob, né le 12 juillet 1902 à Drohobrcy (Pologne), a été interné au Fort de Montluc à LYON, en octobre 1943 et fusillé par les Allemands à l'Ecole de Santé Militaire le 24 novembre 1943 —Acte de décès n° 1049 établi par la Mairie du 7éme Arrondissement -.

     Je vous autorise à vous servir de cette lettre pour la constitution d'un dossier aministratif.

     Veuillez agréer, Madame, mes respectueuses salutations

POUR LE PRÉFET DU RHONE:
Le Chef de Bureau délégué,

Madame HALAUNBRENNER
25, rue des Rossiers
PARIS IVe

S/Couvert de Monsieur le Préfet de Police à Paris.

MONTPELLIER ?LE 19 Mai 43.

Tél. : BALzac 07-27

Chère Madame, le voyage de Georgy
a été avancé de quelques jours et à l'heure actuelle il est déjà dans l'Ain.Voici
son adresse:Maison d'enfants d'Yzieu,par
Brégnier-Cordon.Pour tout ce qui le concer-
ne adressez-vous maintenant à Madame Zlatir
même adresse.J'ai lui fait suivre le petit
paquet que je viens de recevoir et je vous
prie,chère Madame,avec mes regrets de voir
partir mon petit ami de Chaumont,d'agréer mes meilleurs
sentiments.

Montpellier,le 14-V-43.

Cher Monsieur,j'ai reçu votre lettre ce matin
et je m'empresse de vous répondre.Georgy quitte le
de Montpellier et s'en va dimanche,après-demain,dans le
département de l'Ain.Voila sa future adresse : Maison d'enfants d'Yzieu par Bregnier-Cordon (AIN).Il sera là-bas
le personnel de l'ancienne maison de Lodève,c.à.d. dans
conditions que vous avez déjà pu apprécier et où les éduca-
teurs le connaissent et l'aiment bien.Georgy a conservé son
bon caractère qui le fait gâter par tout le monde et de ce
façon il n'est jamais bien malheureux.

Ce le dernier de mes petits amis de Chaumont qui me
quitte.Je le regrettrai d'autant plus qu'il se plaisait be
coup à Montpellier où il est dans des conditions materiell
morales et de sécurité tout-à-fait exceptionnelles.

Georges Halpern

Birth date: October 30, 1935   Birthplace: Vienna, Austria

Seraphine Friedmann Halpern, born September 23, 1907, in Vienna, was separated from her only child, Georges, due to ill health; she was hospitalized at Saint-Louis Hospital in Perpignan, then at the sanatorium L'Espérance in Hauteville, near Izieu in the department of Ain. Georges was sheltered first at the OSE children's home in the Château de Chaumont at Mainsat in the department of Creuse, then at the home in Campestre à Lodève, which OSE shut down at the beginning of August 1943.

It is thanks to Georges, who wrote regularly to his parents, that we have a picture of life at Izieu.

Monday, January 17, 1944

Dear Mommy,

I got your card, and it made me very happy. I am fine, and I'm having a good time. At our Christmas party, we put on skits and we had good things to eat: we ate gingerbread, chocolate, quince jam, and a bag of candy, and we drank Ovaltine. We also got toys. I got a tin of watercolors and a sketch pad.

Are you feeling all right? The little New Year's card was very pretty, I already wrote back to Daddy. There's no snow yet, I'm eating well, I'm sleeping well, I'm fine, we go for hikes on Thursdays and Sundays. We get up at seven, in the morning we have coffee with bread and jam, for lunch sometimes soup, vegetables, dessert, for afternoon snacks we have milk with bread and chocolate, for supper soup, vegetables, and yogurt. Your son who loves you very much sends you 1000000000000 kisses.

There are high mountains, and the village is very pretty. There are lots of farms, sometimes we go for a walk to Bregnier-Cordon. The house is very nice, we pick mulberries and blackberries and redberries. I love you with all my heart.

Georgy

Monday, February 7, 1944

Dear Mommy,

I got your letter and the photo, which I liked very much. Saturday there was snow, it's not real cold yet, there's a big terrace where you can see the whole landscape and it's very pretty to see all the mountains covered with snow. I need underpants and socks, the director said you'd send me 100 francs because she has a coupon to buy shoes. Are you feeling well? I'm fine, I'm eating well and I'm having fun and I'm feeling well. Your son who loves you very much sends you 1000000000 kisses.

Georgy

Georgy was deported in convoy number seventy-one. His parents live today in Israel and are associate plaintiffs.

Top: Georges Halpern. Above: Excerpt of a letter from Georges Halpern to his mother.

Opposite, below and above: Letters from an OSE official, Mr. Annenkov, to the parents of Georges Halpern.

Montpellier, May 14, 1943

Dear Sir,

I received your letter this morning, and I hasten to respond. Georgy is leaving the region of Montpellier on Sunday afternoon for the department of Ain. His future address: Children's home at Yzieu [sic], near Bregnier-Cordon, Ain. There, he will be with the staff of the former home at Lodève, that is, in conditions which are already familiar to you and where the supervisors know and like him. Georgy is as good-natured as ever, to the point that everyone spoils him and, in this way, he is never really unhappy.

He is the last of my little friends from Chaumont to leave me. I will miss him all the more, as he very much enjoyed himself in Montpellier, where he has been in conditions which, both materially and from the point of view of morale and security, have been quite exceptional.

Montpellier, May 19, 1943

Dear Madame,

Georgy's voyage was advanced a few days, and at this very moment he is already in the department of Ain. Here is his address: Children's home at Yzieu [sic], near Bregnier-Cordon. For all that concerns him, you may now address yourself to Mrs. Zlatin at the same address. I have forwarded to him the small package which I just received. With regrets at seeing my little friend from Chaumont depart, I am, dear Madame,

Sincerely yours.

Arnold Hirsch

Birth date: March 23, 1927   Birthplace: Argenschwang, Germany

Arnold's parents—Ida Harf Hirsch, born December 3, 1900, in Seibersbach, Germany, and Max Hirsch, born October 8, 1898, in Argenschwang—were deported in the same convoy as the parents of his cousin Egon Gamiel, who was also at Izieu. Arnold, who had assumed the identity of Jean-Pierre Barreau, was deported with his best friend, Théo Reis, and with Mr. Zlatin on May 15, 1944, in convoy number seventy-three. This all-male convoy was first sent to Kaunas, Lithuania, where half its number remained and were quickly wiped out by the SS in the town's citadel or in the camp at Projanowski. The remainder of the convoy was sent on to Tallinn, Estonia, incarcerated in the citadel, and murdered by the SS practically to the last man.

Doris Harf, the first cousin of Arnold's mother, is associate plaintiff on her cousins' behalf.

Théo Reis (left) and Arnold Hirsch (right) with Paulette Paillarès, their friend from Montpellier. Most of the photographs from Izieu were taken in the summer of 1943 by Paulette, who was devoted to the children there.

Isidore Kargeman

Birth date: March 29, 1934   Birthplace: Paris, France

Isidore's father, Szloma Kargeman, was born July 10, 1900, in Grodno, Russia (now Poland); he was deported on June 5, 1942, to Auschwitz, where he was murdered. Isidore's mother was Sonia Siderka.

Isidore was deported in convoy number seventy-one. His brother is associate plaintiff.

Above left: Birth certificate of Isidore Kargeman. Above right: Isidore Kargeman before his arrival at Izieu.

Renate Krochmal

Birth date: September 3, 1935   Birthplace: Vienna, Austria

Liane Krochmal

Birth date: July 25, 1937   Birthplace: Vienna, Austria

Renate and Liane's father, Jacob, born November 1, 1896, in
Brody, Poland, and mother, Amalie born January 19, 1908, in
Vienna, were interned at Rivesaltes, then turned over by Vichy to
the SS. They were deported on September 16, 1942, in convoy
number thirty-three to Auschwitz, where both were murdered.
Their eldest child, Siegfried, died at Rivesaltes in 1942, at the age
of eleven.

Renate and Liane were deported in convoy number seventy-
one. Their father's brother and sister, Henry and Klara, live in the
United States and are associate plaintiffs.

Siegfried, Renate, and Liane Krochmal (opposite), and their parents (above). All five family
members perished as a result of the Final
Solution.

DAS BABi SCHICKT VIELE PUSSI

lieber oncel, tante & und
Klara ich ~~mich~~ möchte schon
gerne in Amerika sein Pussi

renate Krochmal

Little Renate hoped to leave France for the safety of the United States, as shown in the short, handwritten excerpt at left: "Dear Uncle, Auntie, and Klara, I so wish I were already in America. Pussi [apparent nickname of Liane]. Renate Krochmal." However, the Krochmal family was refused an entry visa by the United States Department of State (below). Three years later, OSE notified Henry Krochmal, the children's uncle, of the fate of his nephew and nieces (opposite).

Visa Form R-3

DEPARTMENT OF STATE
WASHINGTON

In reply refer to
VD 811.111 Krochmal, Jacob

July 31, 1942.

Mr. Heinrich Krochmal,
95 Lenox Road,
Brooklyn, New York.

Sir:

Reference is made to your interest in the application for a permit to enter the United States in the case of Jacob Krochmal and his family.

This case has been carefully considered by an Interdepartmental Committee, by an Interdepartmental Visa Review Committee and by the Board of Appeals in the light of the provisions of section 58.47 of the regulations covering the control of persons entering and leaving the United States pursuant to the Act of May 22, 1918, as amended. The conclusion has been reached that a favorable recommendation for the issuance of a visa may not be sent to the appropriate consular officer.

Section 58.57(g) of the aforementioned regulations provides that the Board of Appeals may not reconsider any case until after the lapse of a period of six months from the date of the previous opinion of the board in the case concerned, and section 58.57(f) provides that only the recommendation of the committee or board, without reasons therefor, shall be disclosed.

Very truly yours,

H. K. Travers
Chief, Visa Division

May 25, 1945.

Mr. Henry Krochmal
118 East 96th St.
Brooklyn, N.Y.

Dear Mr. Krochmal :

It is with a feeling of deepest sadness that we are transmitting to you the cable information we have received from our Swiss office that your nephew, Siegfried Krochmal is dead since 1942, and that your nieces, Liane and Renate were deported in 1944.

The dreadful calamity which has befallen the Jewish people is of such huge proportions that the individual sorrow and bereavement must be submerged in the common grief. However, one should continue to hope in the light of recent liberation of deportees by Allied armies.

Yours most sincerely,

L. Wulman, MD

Secretary

a-g

Max Leiner

Birth date: February 26, 1936   Birthplace: Mannheim, Germany

Max's mother had entrusted him to her own mother. The child was deported in convoy number seventy-one. His mother's sister, who lives in Israel, is an associate plaintiff.

Max Leiner

Claude Levan-Reifman

Birth date: July 11, 1933   Birthplace: Paris, France

Claude's mother, Dr. Suzanne Levan-Reifman, was the physician at Izieu, where her parents, Moïse and Eva Reifman, were residing as well. All four were deported in convoy number seventy-one.

Claude's uncle, Dr. Léon Reifman, who escaped the raid, is associate plaintiff on behalf of the family.

Opposite, above: Back row center, Fritz Löbmann; front row center, Otto Wertheimer, Fritz's cousin. Opposite, below: Fritz Löbmann was in possession of 480 francs when he arrived at Drancy with the other children from Izieu, according to card number 114 of the camp's body-search records. His last address —Izieu—is noted, as well as the party responsible for his transfer to Drancy: the German police in Lyon (*de P.A. Lyon*, "P.A." standing for *Police Allemande*).

Fritz Löbmann

Birth date: March 12, 1929   Birthplace: Mannheim, Germany

Fritz's mother, Mathilde Wertheimer Löbmann, was born April 8, 1899, in Kettel, Germany; she was deported August 17, 1942, in convoy number twenty for Auschwitz, where she was murdered.

The cousin of Otto Wertheimer, who was also at Izieu, Fritz worked under the name of François Loban on a nearby farm. Both he and Otto were deported in convoy number seventy-one.

Cousins in Strasbourg, France, and in Israel are associate plaintiffs on behalf of both Fritz Löbmann and Otto Wertheimer.

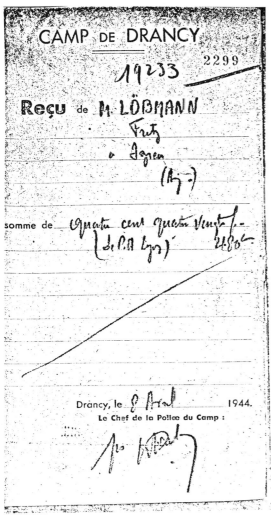

Alice-Jacqueline Luzgart

Birth date: October 8, 1933   Birthplace: Paris, France

Alice-Jacqueline's father, Nahoum Luzgart, was born March 3, 1886, in Odessa, Russia; he died just before the outbreak of World War II. Her mother, Sarah, was also originally from Russia. On April 1, 1944, little Alice-Jacqueline wrote to her sister Fanny:

My dearest sister,

I was very glad to get your letter, dated the 28th.

Did you get the letter I sent asking you for lots of candy canes and some tins of hard licorice? I hope you got it and do your best to get me the other things I asked you for, too: paper, envelopes, and ten stamps.

You know, today is April 1st and it's also April Fools' Day, when they pin fish on your back.* This morning, they stuck two on me at once, but I noticed them.

I chose accountant, but, you know, my girlfriend chose a nicer profession than I did, she wants to be a student-midwife in the maternity ward when she grows up. She told me she'd like to operate on the mothers to bring little children into the world because she likes little babies. Don't you think that's a fine profession? Maybe I'll change my mind and copy her.

Tell me what you wanted to do when you were little. Fanny, I'm sending you a composition topic from last week. Here it is: "One of your relatives is a prisoner, or one of your friends. You sense from his letters his homesickness for his native land. Write to him about France, about his city or town, pick the details that will interest him, the words that will bring him comfort and joy." I scored six-and-a-half. The best grade I've had.

Alice-Jacqueline was deported on May 30, 1944, in convoy number seventy-five. Her sister and niece are associate plaintiffs.

*A French April Fools' Day tradition is cutting out paper fish and pinning them surreptitiously on others' backs.

Alice-Jacqueline Luzgart

Samedi le 26 février 1944

Très chère maman.

J'ai bien reçu ta lettre datée du 18 qui m'a fait grand plaisir.

J'espère que tu as bien reçu ma lettre que je t'ai envoyée il y a quelques jours, à la Taquière.

Je suis en bonne santé et j'espère qu'il en est de même pour toi ainsi que pour Monsieur et Madame Barbier.

Je te remercie d'avoir cherché pour moi des sabots et j'aurai bien chaud chaud n'est ce pas maman.

Ici la neige fond, et le soleil se fait voir, nous voyons bien que le printemps va bientôt venir, quelle chance c'est si joli le printemps avec ses arbres en fleurs aussi ses bourgeons.

Je pense que tu as reçu la lettre dans laquelle je te demande de prendre des photos de là - bas car je ne me rappelle plus comment est le pays, mais il ne faut pas oublier que j'étais bien petite lorsque j'y étais.

Comme tu me l'as dit je donne un grand bonjour à Madame Bouvresse.

Je serai très contente un jour de lui écrire une petite lettre, je suis persuadée que cela lui ferait plaisir n'est ce pas ma chère petite maman, ainsi que tante Henriette.

Je vais recevoir un colis de Fanny avec la jupe à carreaux bleus.

Comme je ne vois plus rien à te dire je te quitte en t'embrassant de toutes mes forces. Bien le bonjour à Mou et Madame Barbier.

Ta petite fille qui pense à toi.

Jacqueline

C00042   Divers - Gagnier

22 Mai 1944.

Monsieur,

[handwritten letter, partially legible]

P. Gagnier

Pasteur P. Gagnier
41 B^d Dubouchage
Nice

C00043

25 Mai 1944

N° 19374
DG/JZ

Le Directeur Général
à
Monsieur le Pasteur
P. GAGNIER
41, boulevard Dubouchage
NICE (A.M.)

Monsieur le Pasteur,

J'ai l'honneur de vous accuser réception de votre lettre du 22 mai.

La Maison à laquelle vous faites allusion n'appartenait pas à mon Etablissement Public. Aussi, je ne suis pas en mesure de vous donner les précisions que vous auriez souhaité avoir.

Je crois, toutefois, savoir que les pensionnaires de cette Maison sont tous partis pour une destination inconnue.

Je vous prie d'agréer, Monsieur le Pasteur, l'assurance de mes sentiments distingués.

Opposite: Letter from Alice-Jacqueline Luzgart to her mother:

Saturday, February 26, 1944

Dearest Mommy,

It made me very happy to get your letter of the 18th.

I hope you have gotten the letter I sent you a few days ago at la Tagnière.

I am in good health, and I hope the same goes for you as well as for Mr. and Mrs. Barbier.

Thank you for picking up clogs for me and I'll be nice and warm, won't I, Mommy.

The snow is melting here, and the sun is peeking through, we can see that spring is sure to be here soon. What luck, spring is so pretty, with its trees and flowers, also its buds. I imagine you have gotten the letter in which I asked you to take some photos of where you are, because I no longer remember what the country is like, but you mustn't forget that I was really little when I was there.

Like you told me, I'm sending kind regards to Mrs. Bouvresse.

I will be very happy to write her a little note one day, I'm convinced that it would make her happy,

don't you think so, my dear little Mommy, as well as Aunt Henriette.

I am going to get a package from Fanny with the blue checked shirt.

Since I can't find anything else to tell you, I will say good-bye, hugging you with all my might. Do give my regards to Mr. and Mrs. Barbier.

Your little daughter, who is thinking of you.

Jacqueline

The Reformed minister in Nice, contacted by Alice-Jacqueline's family, wrote the letter above left to inquire about the girl's fate; to its right is the response of the director general of UGIF South.

May 22, 1944

Sir,

Would you be able to tell me what has become of the following child: Alice Luzgart, who two months ago was at the home for children at Izieu, near Bregnier-Cordon in Ain. There is no word from her. It seems that this home has been split up.

I would be very appreciative if you could obtain some detailed information for me on the current circumstances of this child, and possibly supply me with her address.

You have my heartfelt gratitude in advance.

P. Gagnier

May 25, 1944

The Director General
to
The Reverend P. Gagnier
41, boulevard Dubouchage
Nice (Alpes-Maritimes)

Reverend,

I have the honor of acknowledging receipt of your letter of May 22.

The home to which you refer did not belong to the public institution with which I am associated. Nor am I in a position to provide you with the details which you would have liked.

Nevertheless, I have reason to believe that the residents of this home have all left for an unknown destination.

Very truly yours.

Paula Mermelstein

Birth date: January 10, 1934   Birthplace: Antwerp, Belgium

Marcel Mermelstein

Birth date: January 14, 1937   Birthplace: Antwerp, Belguim

The children's father, Max Mermelstein, was born September 14, 1907, in Mihailovze, Czechoslovakia; he left in 1925 for Antwerp, where he was a kosher butcher. Their mother, Frieda, was born March 6, 1912, in Warsaw. The family moved to Borgerhout, a suburb of Antwerp, then fled to France on May 14, 1940, when the Germans invaded Belgium. The Mermelsteins were interned in Rivesaltes on June 28, 1942.

The children's father managed to join the partisans, while their mother settled in the southwest of France; the children themselves were brought to Izieu in 1943. After their arrest, Frieda Mermelstein was arrested in turn at Pau, possibly because her address had been found at Izieu. She was thus reunited with her children at Drancy, and all three were deported on May 20, 1944, in convoy number seventy-four for Auschwitz, where they were murdered.

Max Mermelstein, who now lives in Australia, is an associate plaintiff.

Top left: Paula Mermelstein. Top right: Marcel Mermelstein. Above: Frieda Mermelstein. All three were deported in convoy number seventy-four to Auschwitz.

Theodor Reis

Birth date: March 19, 1928   Birthplace: Egelsbach, Germany

Théo's mother, Erna Reis, was born July 8, 1905, in Pfaffen-Beerfurth, Germany. She brought him to the home of cousins, the Kahn family, in Wollenberg, Germany; however, the Kahns left for Palestine in 1939. In October 1940, the Jews of the Rhineland were deported to France and thrown into camps in the Free Zone. Théo's mother and grandmother (Johanna, born February 10, 1882, in Pfaffen-Beerfurth) were interned at Rivesaltes and deported August 14, 1942, in convoy number nineteen to Auschwitz, where they were murdered.

Théo and his companion Paul Niederman were together at the OSE children's home at Palavas-les-Flots; the OSE center at Vic-sur-Cère and the Jewish vocational school at Laroche, both in central France; and at Izieu.

Théo was deported with his best friend, Arnold Hirsch, and with Mr. Zlatin, in convoy number seventy-three on May 15, 1944. The three were summarily executed either at Kaunas, Lithuania, or at Tallinn, Estonia.

A cousin living in Israel is associate plaintiff on Théo's behalf.

Top and above: Three photographs of Théo Reis, including one on the terrace at Izieu. Far left: Théo Reis's birth certificate. Left: Death certificate for Théo Reis, dated 1961. Below: Authentication for Théo's death certificate, issued in 1984.

Nr. 447

Berlin, den ___5. Januar___ 19⁶¹

Theodor R e i s , – – – – – – – – – – – – – – – –

Beruf unbekannt, – – – – – – – – – – – – – – – – –

– –

zuletzt wohnhaft in ___Wollenberg, Kreis Sinsheim,___ – – – – –

– –

ist durch Entscheidung des Amtsgerichts ___Neckarbischofsheim___ – – – –

– –

vom ___5. Januar 1960 – II 19/60___ – – – – – – – – – – –

für tot erklärt worden.

Als Zeitpunkt des Todes ist der ___31. Dezember 1945___ – – – – – – – –

– festgestellt.

Der ___ Genannte ist am ___19. März 1928___ – – – – – – – – – – –

in ___Egelsbach, Kreis Offenbach/Main,___ – – – – – – – – geboren.

Der Standesbeamte
In Vertretung

Bauder

Diese Ablichtung gilt als beglaubigte Abschrift. Die Übereinstimmung mit den Eintragungen im Buch für Todeserklärungen des Standesamts I in Berlin (West) wird hiermit beglaubigt.

Berlin, den **27. APRIL 1984**
Der Standesbeamte

Gilles Sadowski

Birth date: September 11, 1935   Birthplace: Paris, France

Gilles's mother, Ruchla Grinfogel Sadowski, was born September 15, 1903, in Warsaw; she was arrested during the Vélodrome d'Hiver raid in Paris in July 1942 and deported July 27, 1942, in convoy number eleven to Auschwitz, where she was murdered. Gilles's father, Symcha Sadowski, living under a false identity, was arrested in Lyon several weeks before the liberation, deported under his false name, and murdered.

Gilles was deported in convoy number seventy-one. His brother Joseph and paternal uncle Chaïm are associate plaintiffs on his behalf.

Above: Gilles Sadowski with his cousin Lili Grinvogel. Lili was deported on August 27, 1942, in convoy number twenty-four; her parents and two sisters were deported as well. Left: Gilles Sadowski's father and mother. Below: Birth certificate of Gilles Sadowsky.

Le onze septembre mil neuf cent trente-cinq, treize heures cinquante-cinq, est né, rue Santerre 15, Gilles, du sexe masculin, de Symcha * SADOWSKI, né à Varsovie (Pologne) en mil huit cent quatre vingt-dix-sept, tricoteur et de Ruchla GRINFOGEL, née à Varsovie, le quinze septembre mil neuf cent trois, sans profession, son épouse, domiciliés à Paris, rue Saint Maur 106. Dressé le douze septembre mil neuf cent * trente-cinq, dix-sept heures vingt, sur la déclaration de Albert GELLY quarante-six ans, employé, domicilié rue Santerre 15, ayant assisté à l'accouchement, qui, lecture faite, a signé avec Nous, Marie-Léon BRIL-LIÉ, adjoint au Maire du douzième arrondissement de Paris, Chevalier de la Légion d'Honneur./.

Martha Spiegel

Birth date: September 27, 1933   Birthplace: Vienna, Austria

Senta Spiegel

Birth date: March 30, 1935   Birthplace: Vienna, Austria

The girls' father, Aron Spiegel, was born May 25, 1910, in Podhajce, Austria (now USSR); their mother, Rachel Vogelbaum Spiegel, was born June 10, 1907, in Skalat, Austria (now USSR). The family's address in Vienna was Pernerstorfergasse 78. Having fled to France and been interned by Vichy, the parents were deported September 25, 1942, in convoy number thirty-seven to Auschwitz, where Rachel Spiegel was murdered. Aron Spiegel survived the camp and learned in 1945 that his daughters had been deported in convoy number seventy-one.

Bertha, the girls' maternal aunt, lives in the United States and is associate plaintiff on their behalf.

Sigmund Springer

Birth date: March 15, 1936   Birthplace: Vienna, Austria

Mendel Lazar Springer, Sigmund's father, was born January 3, 1906, in Tarnow, Poland; his mother, Sarah Leifer Springer, was born November 2, 1901, in Madworna, Poland. Both parents, interned at Rivesaltes and handed over by Vichy to the SS, were deported September 11, 1942, in convoy number thirty-one to Auschwitz, where they were murdered.

Sigmund was deported in convoy number seventy-one. Cousins who live in Israel are associate plaintiffs on Sigmund's behalf.

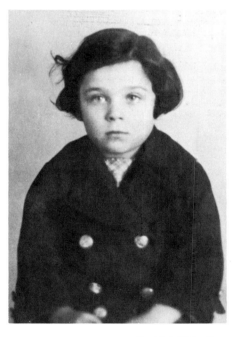

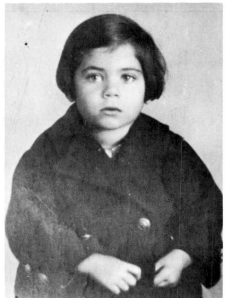

Martha Spiegel

Senta Spiegel

Sarah Szulklaper

Birth date: February 5, 1933   Birthplace: Paris, France

Sarah's mother, Tauba Klinger Szulklaper, was born May 30, 1910, in Radour, Poland; her father, Huna Szulklaper, was born December 7, 1912. Both parents were deported on July 18, 1943, in convoy number fifty-seven to Auschwitz, where they were murdered.

Sarah, who preferred to be called Suzanne, was deported in convoy number seventy-one. Her paternal uncle, who lives in Australia, is associate plaintiff on her behalf.

In honor of Sarah (Suzanne) Szulklaper's eleventh birthday, February 5, 1944, six of her friends at Izieu wrote her letters:

My dear Suzanne,
   I wish you a very happy birthday, and hope that next year you'll be with your parents. Our gifts may be small, but my wishes for you are big. I'll leave room for the others.
                  Mina [Nina Aronowicz]

My dear Suzanne,
   I wish you a happy birthday, and that you'll rejoin your parents and spend your birthday with them next year. My warm wishes for your eleventh birthday.
                  Senta [Senta Spiegel]

Dear Suzanne,
   I wish you a happy birthday in honor of your eleven years. I hope you'll like this present, but it's not a big one.
                  Martha [Martha Spiegel]

Dear Suzanne,
   I'm writing this little note to make you happy on your birthday. Hoping you rejoin your parents and that the war gets over. To my dear Suzanne,
                  Esther [Esther Benassayag]

Dear Suzanne,
   On the occasion of your birthday, we're all writing to you to make you happy. It's today, on this day, which unfortunately is not like the other birthdays. I close this little note by wishing that on your next birthday, you'll have your parents back. HAPPY BIRTHDAY.
                  Liliane [Liliane Gerenstein]

My dearest Suzanne,
   Today is the day we wish you a happy eleventh birthday. I hope that next year's, as well as all the others, will take place at your parents' house, and that you will be home with them again soon. I close with a great big hug.
   Your friend who will never forget you,
                  Alice [Alice-Jacqueline Luzgart]

Left: Sarah Szulklaper and her father, Huna. Both were murdered at Auschwitz, as was Sarah's mother, Tauba. Below: Birth certificate (left) and death certificate (right) of Sarah Szulklaper.

Le dix février mil neuf cent trente-trois, treize heures, est née, 17 rue Dieu, Sarah, du sexe féminin, de Tauba KLINGER, née à Radour (Eologne), en mil neuf cent dix, sans profession, domiciliée à Paris, 28 rue de Belleville.- Dressé le onze février mil neuf cent trente-trois, dix-sept heures cinq, sur la déclara-tion de Alfred Gayet, cinquante-quatre ans, employé, au domicile duquel l'ac-couchement a eu lieu, qui, lecture faite, a signé avec Nous, Paul DUBOIS, Ad-joint au Maire du dixième arrondissement de Paris, Chevalier de la Légion d' Honneur./.

Max Tetelbaum

Birth date: August 14, 1931 **Birthplace: Antwerp, Belgium**

Herman Tetelbaum

Birth date: November 1, 1933 **Birthplace: Antwerp, Belgium**

Sons of Jankiel Tetelbaum, born in 1900 in Ostrow, Russia, and Sefa Silberberg Tetelbaum, born in 1901 in Lublin, Poland, the boys were deported to Auschwitz in convoy number seventy-one under the names Max and Armand Teitel. As in the case of the Mermelsteins, the boys' arrest led to the discovery of their family's address, either through the seizure of letters addressed to them at Izieu or as a result of the interrogations at Fort Montluc or Drancy. This in turn led to the arrest of their mother, their sister (Gabrielle, born October 2, 1927, in Antwerp), and their brother (Maurice, born November 27, 1929, in Antwerp). From the records of body-searches at Drancy, we have ascertained that the three were arrested in Chambéry, where they lived at 42 faubourg Montmélian, and that the arrest is likely to have taken place a very short time before their transfer to Drancy on April 21. The mother, deported under the name of Charlotte, and her two elder children left Drancy on April 29, 1944, in convoy number seventy-two, which immediately followed that of Max and Herman; like the two younger boys, they were murdered in Auschwitz.

Of this family of six, only the father escaped deportation and murder. Max and Herman's paternal aunt, who lives in Israel near Haifa, is an associate plaintiff on their behalf.

Opposite: Sefa and Jankiel Tetelbaum with their children (left to right), Herman, Maurice, Gabrielle, and Max, in 1935. Ten years later only the father was still alive. Below left: Excerpts from the rosters from convoy number seventy-one and convoy number seventy-two. Below right: The birth certificates of Max and Herman Tetelbaum.

Charles Weltner

Birth date: August 7, 1934   Birthplace: Paris, France

Charles was the son of Joseph Weltner, born March 13, 1910, in Kemeneshogyesz, Hungary, and Marguerite Landsman Weltner, born November 20, 1910, in Budapest.

Charles was deported on May 30, 1944, in convoy number seventy-five. His mother lives in Paris.

Above: Birth certificate of Charles Weltner, reissued in 1984. Right: Charles Weltner with his father before the war.

Otto Wertheimer

. . . .

Birth date: February 5, 1932   Birthplace: Baden-Württemberg, Germany

. . . .

Otto's father, Wilhelm Wertheimer, was born July 8, 1890, in Kettel, Germany; his mother, Hedwig Lederman Wertheimer, was born March 11, 1901, in Mannheim, Germany. Both parents were deported from Germany and interned in Gurs in the Free Zone in October 1940; after transfer from Gurs to Drancy, they left on August 17, 1942, in convoy number twenty for Auschwitz, where they were murdered.

The cousin of Fritz Löbmann, who was also at Izieu, Otto was deported in convoy number seventy-one under a false identity, Octave Wermet. Two cousins, one living in Strasbourg, France, the other in Israel, are associate plaintiffs on both Otto's behalf and that of Fritz Löbmann.

207 - WERTHEIMER Hedwig - II.3.OI Mannheim	Allemande	3.P.
208 - WERTHEIMER Wilheim - 8.7.90 Kettl	"	Commerçant
209 - LOBMANN Mathilde 8.4.99 Ketti	Ex-Allemande	3.P.
née WERTHEIMER		

Top: In this photograph from Izieu, Otto Wertheimer is front row right on one knee. Above: Both of Otto Wertheimer's parents and the mother of Fritz Löbmann were deported in car number nine, convoy number twenty, to Auschwitz, as this excerpt from the roster shows.

Emile Zuckerberg

Birth date: May 15, 1938   Birthplace: Antwerp, Belgium

Emile was the son of Zygmund Zuckerberg, born August 25, 1903, in Stara Wies, Poland, and of Serla Rosenfeld Zuckerberg, born December 30, 1906, in Kamionka, Poland. After internment at Rivesaltes, both parents were deported September 14, 1942, in convoy thirty-three to Auschwitz, where they were murdered.

Emile, deported in convoy number seventy-one, was torn from the arms of Léa Feldblum during the selection and pushed into the line leading to the gas chamber. Emile's cousin, Adolf Zuckerberg, lives in Israel and is an associate plaintiff.

Right: Emile Zuckerberg (standing, first row, in white shorts) at Izieu. Below: Legal declaration of death for Emile Zuckerberg and his parents, dated April 12, 1957. According to the certificate, issued by the mayor of the Antwerp suburb Berchem, all three died at "an unknown location."

AKTE NR 170

De eerste Juli duizend negenhonderd zeven en vijftig, te 11.00 uur, is door Ons, Robert Bossaerts, Burgemeester, Ambtenaar van de Burgerlijke Stand van de gemeente Berchem,provincie Antwerpen, volgend beschikkend gedeelte van een vonnis van verklaring van overlijden,van de Rechtbank van eerste aanleg zitting houdende te Antwerpen, op ~~acht en twintig~~ twaalf April duizend negenhonderd zeven en vijftig, hetwelk hieraan zal gehecht blijven, na korttekening overgeschreven: - - - - - - - - - - - - - -
De Rechtbank viegt de verzoekschriften samen en rechtdoende, verklaart dat: 1° Rosenfeld Serla Chaja, geboren te Kamionka in Polen, op dertig december duizend negenhonderd en zes, dochter van Peibisch Rosenfeld en van Etie Gittel Nachtgeist, naaister van beroep, echtgenote van Zygmunt Zuckerberg,laatst gehuisvest te Berchem, Gitschotellei, nummer honderd zeven en zestig, overleden is op zestien september duizend negenhonderd twee en veertig, te vier en twintig uur, in een onbekende plaats. -------
2° Zuckerberg Emiel, geboren te Antwerpen op viftien mei duizend negenhonderd acht en dertig, zoon van Zygmunt Zuckerberg en van Serla Chaja Rosenfeld, zonder beroep,ongehuwd,laatst gehuisvest te Berchem, Gitschotellei nummer honderd zeven en zestig,overleden is op dertien april duizend negenhonderd vier en veertig, te vier en twintig uur, in een onbekende plaats.- 3° Zuckerberg Zygmunt, geboren te Stara-Wies in Polen, op vijf en twintig augustus duizend negenhonderd en drie, zoon van Chaja Rijfka Zuckerberg, diamantsnijder van beroep, echtgenoot van Serla Chaja Rosenfeld, laatst gehuisvest te Berchem, Gitschotellei nummer honderd zeven en zestig, overleden is op zestien September duizend negenhonderd twee en veertig, te vier en twintig uur, in een onbekende plaats. Stelt de onmogelijkheid vast deplaats van het overlijden in de overlijdensakte te vermelden. Beveelt dat het beschikkend gedeelte van het huidig vonnis van verklaring van overlijden, wanneer het kracht van gewijsde zal bekomen hebben zal overgeschreven worden in de lopende registers van de Burgerlijke Stand van de gemeente Berchem.Beveelt dat er melding zal van gemaakt worden in de jaarlijkse en tien jaarlijkse tabellen der registers van het jaar van overlijden, ter griffie en ter gemeente berustend. Zegt dat de ambtenaar van de Burgerlijke Stand der laatste woon---plaats zich zal gedragen naar de bepalingen van art. 79 van het Burgerlijk Wetboek, aangevuld door artikel 11 der wet van 16 December 1851, op straf van de bij dit artikel voorziene geldboeten. Zegt dat het vonnis als akte van overlijden zal gelden en aan derden zal kunnen tegengesteld worden. Goedgekeurd de doorhaling van drie woorden Voor eensluidend afschrift, de ambtenaar in hoofde dezer vermeld.- - - - - - - - -

THE ADULTS

Those Who Were Deported and Murdered

Lucie Feiger

Birth date: June 7, 1894   Birthplace: Metz, Germany (now France)

Lucie Feiger was deported in convoy number seventy-one.

Mina Friedler

Birth date: February 20, 1912   Birthplace: Turku, Poland

Mina Kunstler Friedler lived at Izieu with her daughter, Lucienne, with whom she was deported on June 30, 1944, in convoy number seventy-six.

Sarah (Suzanne) Levan-Reifman

Birth date: August 20, 1907   Birthplace: Sagani, Rumania

Moïse Reifman

Birth date: April 12, 1881   Birthplace: Sagani, Rumania

Eva Reifman

Birth date: March 14, 1883   Birthplace: Baramcia, Rumania

Dr. Sarah Levan-Reifman came to Izieu with her son, Claude, and her parents, Moïse and Eva Reifman, following the departure of her brother, Léon. All four were deported in convoy number seventy-one.

Dr. Léon Reifman is associate plaintiff on behalf of the family.

Miron Zlatin

Birth date: September 21, 1904   Birthplace: Orcha, Russia

A distinguished agronomist, Mr. Zlatin looked after the welfare of the children in every possible way. He was beloved by all.

Mr. Zlatin was deported in convoy number seventy-three on May 15, 1944.

Opposite: On the front steps of the house at Izieu, clockwise from upper left, are Marcelle Endlich, a counselor who left Izieu several months before the raid; Dr. Suzanne Levan-Reifman; Miron Zlatin; and Mrs. Mering, a devoted friend of the Zlatins and of the children of Izieu.

The Sole Survivor of Deportation

Laja (Léa) Feldblum

Birth date: July 1, 1918   Birthplace: Warsaw, Poland

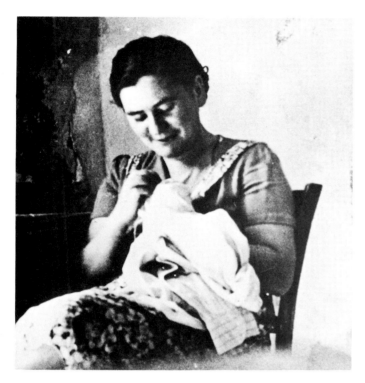

Léa Feldblum sewing at Izieu.

The Feldblum family, which had lived in Antwerp, Belgium, since 1929, fled to the southwest of France in May 1940 and was assigned to residence in the department of Hérault at Bousquet-d'Orb, some thirty-five miles northwest of Montpellier. Léa's parents died in Montpellier, eight months apart; her sister Rywka and brother Moses were deported September 12, 1942, in convoy number thirty-one to Auschwitz, where they were murdered.

Léa worked as a teacher-counselor at the children's homes at Palavas-les-Flots and Campestre à Lodève. She moved to Chambéry, where she continued working for OSE, and finally to the home at Izieu.

In March 1944, when Mrs. Zlatin decided it would be advisable to close down the home and evacuate the children to a less vulnerable location, Léa was granted a safe-conduct by French authorities to escort them from Izieu to Bousquet-d'Orb (see document opposite). Tragically, this move, which Mrs. Zlatin had gone to Montpellier to arrange, was preempted by the Lyon Gestapo's raid.

Léa was arrested at Izieu under an assumed name, Marie-Louise Decoste. After the interrogations at Fort Montluc, she was transferred to Drancy, where she revealed her true identity so that she could be deported with the rest from the home. Léa had already turned down two opportunities to cross into Switzerland; once again, she opted to stick with her children.

Upon arrival at Auschwitz on April 15, Léa was at the head of the children, who were lined up five abreast on the platform. An officer asker her, "Sind das deine Kinder?" (Are those your children?) She answered, "Das ist ein Kinderheim." (This is a children's home.) She was then brutally separated from the children; little Emile Zuckerberg, who adored her and clung to her, was torn from her arms. She would be marked with the number 78620 and would survive—perhaps so that at least one soul might remember, and bear witness to, the fate of the children of Izieu to the very last moment of their martyrdom.

Léa was liberated at Auschwitz in January 1945; she returned to France by way of Odessa.

In 1946 Léa emigrated to Palestine, where she married the same year. Two years later, her husband was killed in the struggle for Israeli independence.

Léa Feldblum has devoted her life to the education of children. She has one daughter and several grandchildren. She is good incarnate.

Opposite: Safe-conduct issued to Léa Feldblum on March 9, 1944, for the purpose of "accompanying children from the home at Izieu" to Bousquet-d'Orb in Hérault. The pass demonstrates that, weeks before the Gestapo raid, measures were being envisaged for breaking up the home at Izieu and moving the children to a safer location.

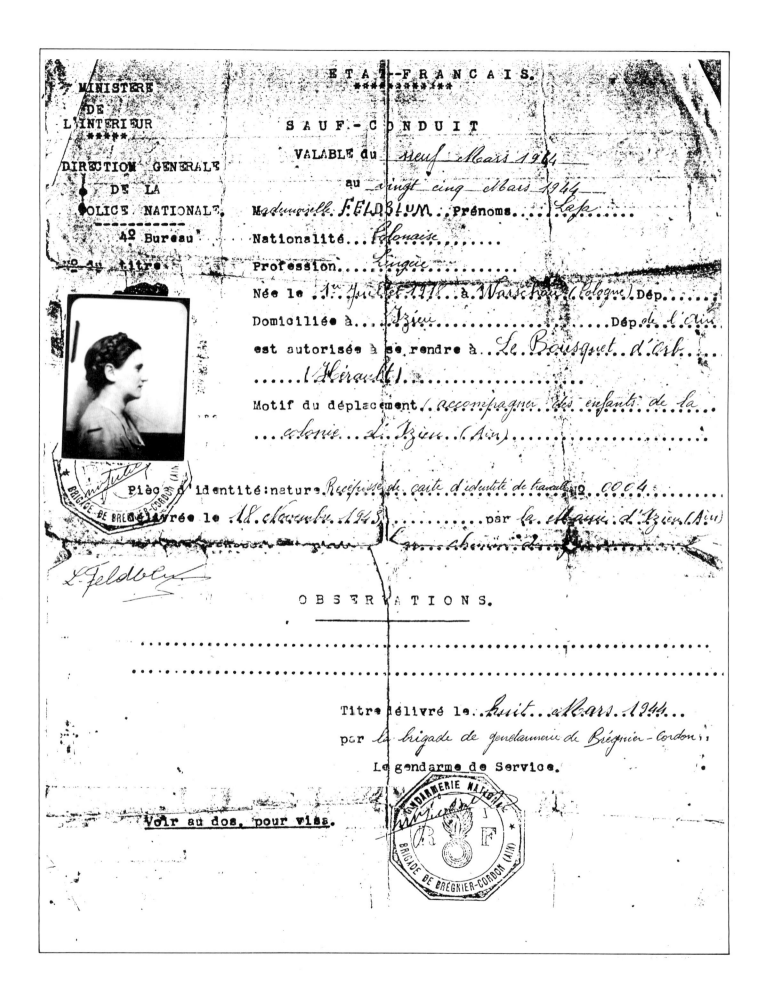

ETAT-FRANCAIS.
****

MINISTERE
DE
L'INTERIEUR
****

DIRECTION GENERALE
DE LA
POLICE NATIONALE

4º Bureau

Nº du titre

S A U F - C O N D U I T

VALABLE du *neuf Mars 1944*

au *vingt cinq Mars 1944*

Mademoiselle *FELDBLUM* Prénoms *Lafa*

Nationalité *Polonaise*

Profession *Lingère*

Née le *1ᵉʳ Juillet 1911* à *Warschau (Pologne)* Dép.

Domiciliée à *Izieu* Dép de *l'Ain*

est autorisée à se rendre à *Le Bousquet d'Orb*

(Hérault)

Motif du déplacement *accompagner les enfants de la*

colonie d'Izieu (Ain)

Pièce d'identité : nature *Récépissé de carte d'identité de travail nº 0004*

délivrée le *18 Novembre 1943* par *la Mairie d'Izieu (Ain)*

Commission de

L. Feldblum

O B S E R V A T I O N S.

....

....

Titre délivré le *huit Mars 1944*

par *la brigade de gendarmerie de Brégnier-Cordon*

Le gendarme de Service.

Voir au dos, pour visa.

Above: Among other Izieu residents is Léa, second from left, kneeling. Right: Mrs. Zlatin's reference letter, attesting to the wartime activities of Léa Feldblum, stamped at bottom left by the French body overseeing repatriation after the war:

I certify by these presents that Miss Léa Feldblum worked in my children's home, under the name of Marie-Louise Decoste.

The "clandestine" children's home was situated in the region of the partisans of Ain, and for this reason was extremely vulnerable. Léa Feldblum, faithful to her post, refused to leave France for Switzerland.

Arrested April 6, 1944, by the SS, with the entire home (the children included), she escaped death and returned from the extermination camp at Auschwitz.

I consider her to be an exemplary member of the Resistance, and call upon the authorities to recognize her as such.

Paris, May 31, 1945

> S. Zlatin
> Former Director of the
> children's home at Izieu, Ain
> Social worker for the
> Resistance in the South Zone
>
> D. Mantoux
> National social worker
> Movement for National
> Liberation, in the South Zone

Je certifie par la présente que Mademoiselle, Léa FELDBLUM a travaillé dans ma maison d'enfants, sous le nom de Marie-Louise Decoste.

La maison d'enfants " clandestine " était située dans la région de maquis de l'Ain, par ce fait extrêmement exposée. Léa FELDBLUM, fidèle à son poste, a refusé de quitter la France pour la Suisse.

Arrêtée le 6 Avril 1944 par les S.S. avec toute la maison(enfants compris), a échappée à la mort et vient du camp d'extermination d'Auchwitz.

Je la considère comme une parfaite résistante, et prie les autorités de la considérer comme telle.

Paris, le 31 Mai 1945

S. ZLATIN

Ex-Directrice de la Maison d'enfants d'Izieu(Ain)
Assistante sociale de la Résistance dans la zone sud.

D. MANTOUX

Assistante sociale nationale
M.L.N., dans la zone Sud

Léon Reifman

Birth date: January 4, 1914   Birthplace: Sagani, Rumania

Before Mrs. Zlatin founded the home at Izieu, Léon Reifman had tried unsuccessfully to enlist the help of the archdiocese of Chambéry in placing children from the home at Palavas-les-Flots—where he had been a counselor—with religious institutions in the Italian zone. A medical student, Léon was medic at Izieu until he became the subject of a search by the forced labor authorities; in September 1943, he left his duties to his sister, Dr. Suzanne Levan-Reifman, and fled to Montpellier. He returned to Izieu on the very morning of the raid, bringing with him two boys from the boarding school they attended in Belley; Max Balsam and Maurice Gerenstein planned to take advantage of Easter recess to visit their brother and sister, respectively. The three arrived by bus at Izieu.

Hardly had Léon been greeted by his parents, sister, and nephew, than the raid took place. When his sister shouted at him to make a run for it, Léon jumped from a second-story window and made good his escape.

After the war, Léon Reifman became a medical doctor. He is associate plaintiff on behalf of his family.

The One Who Escaped the Raid

The following episode, described by Dr. Léon Reifman and reported in the Lyon newspaper *Progrès-Dimanche* on February 13, 1983, took place in the spring of 1943, before the establishment of the home for Jewish children at Izieu:

Dr. Reifman wrote the following to Mr. René Nodot on June 20, 1978: "I was assigned to explore the possibilities for scattering our children among different Christian institutions....I therefore felt that it would be best to address myself to the archbishop of Chambéry.

"I was received by the secretary, a young priest. I laid out for him the object of my visit. Quite agreeably, he told me that he found my request justified and that, undoubtedly, Monsignor would look upon it kindly and that his decision would be favorable. But as he himself was not able to make the decision, he invited me to return later for the answer, as he would take it upon himself to present my request to the archbishop.

"I was about to leave when a large black automobile entered the courtyard of the archbishop's residence. 'Well, now, here's Monsignor. You'll present your request to him yourself,' said the priest.

"I explained in a concise manner the object of my visit, underlining the danger that any delay in their evacuation would hold for the children.

"The tone changed. 'But, sir, how do you expect us to mix Catholic children and Jewish children in our institutions?'

"I allowed myself to observe that in the face of the danger of deportation and death, certain considerations, as justified as they might otherwise be, ought to retreat into the background, particularly as a temporary solution was at issue.

" 'Sir, I will think it over, leave your address, I will write to you.'

"Two days later, I received a card: 'Monsignor Costa de Beauregard regrets that he is not able to make a favorable answer to your request.' "

Léon Reifman on the terrace at Izieu.

René Wucher a vécu la rafle d'Izieu par Barbie :

« Des civils avec de grands manteaux nous ont emmenés »

*Il avait
huit ans en 1944.
Il a été sauvé
au dernier moment*

L E 6 avril 1944, Barbie vint rafler à la colonie d'Izieu (Ain), quarante et un petits pensionnaires juifs et les dix personnes qui composaient le personnel. On ne les revit jamais. Seuls, le docteur Reithmàn (30 ans à l'époque) put sauter par la fenêtre et se cacher, et le petit René Wucher fut libéré quelques kilomètres plus loin, sans savoir pourquoi.

René Wucher (47 ans) a aujourd'hui deux enfants et travaille à la R.A.T.P. En 1944, il avait 8 ans. Les nécessités familiales et économiques de l'époque avaient scindé sa famille en deux. Sa mère et deux de ses frères étaient restés dans la région parisienne. René était allé rejoindre Antoine, son père, avec André, son aîné (10 ans à l'époque).

Antoine, établi mécanicien à

Il fut libéré peu après. On ne revit aucun des 40 enfants et les 10 adultes arrêtés

Murs, à quelques kilomètres d'Izieu, travaillait le plus souvent à domicile chez les cultivateurs de la région. Toute la journée, il parcourait les routes des environs, sur son vélo. René et André Wucher ne manquaient de rien et, autant qu'ils s'en souviennent, ils étaient heureux. Tel était le garçon de 8 ans qui, un beau jour, se retrouva à la colonie d'Izieu.

Un porcelet entre les jambes

« Aujourd'hui encore, raconte-t-il, je ne sais toujours pas pourquoi. Je ne me souviens plus combien de temps j'y suis resté. Sans doute plu-sieurs semaines, parce que mon frère et mon père venaient me voir. De la vie du centre, je n'ai gardé qu'un souvenir imprécis. On nous faisait un peu l'école, pas beaucoup. Le plus souvent, nous étions dehors à jouer dans la cour. »

C'est tout ce qu'un enfant de 8 ans a pu retenir d'une vie jusque-là sans vraies difficultés. Mais le 6 avril 1944 a laissé une empreinte plus profonde dans la mémoire d'André :

« Par la fenêtre, nous avons vu arriver les camions dans la cour. Dedans, il y avait peu de militaires. C'étaient surtout des civils, avec des grands manteaux. Ils se sont éparpillés un peu partout en criant. Le personnel de la colonie est venu nous chercher, puis cela s'est passé très vite. Les enfants et les adultes ont été séparés et moi, je me suis retrouvé au fond d'un petit camion, près du gazogène. Je ne me souviens pas d'avoir reçu des coups. Dehors, derrière mon véhicule, je pouvais apercevoir une grande décapotable avec quatre ou cinq officiers. Celui qui se trouvait près du chauffeur avait un porcelet entre les jambes. C'est une image qui ne m'a jamais quitté. Dans le camion, nous nous sommes mis à chanter, moi comme les autres. Peut-être, pour les plus grands, était-ce une façon de dire quelque chose. Mais pour moi, c'était un chant de promenade. »

Trois kilomètres plus loin, le convoi parvient à La Bruyère, au carrefour de la route d'Izieu.

René Wucher se tait, son regard fait le tour de la pièce, les larmes à fleur de paupière. Sa voix tremble un peu lorsqu'il reprend :

« J'ai toujours eu de la chance, sauf au jeu. C'est peut-être ce jour-là qu'elle s'est attachée à moi. Au carrefour, le convoi s'est arrêté parce qu'un véhicule est tombé en panne. **Mon camion stationnait de-**vant une petite fabrique de confiserie où une de mes cousines travaillait. Lorsqu'elle m'a aperçu, elle s'est trouvée mal. Un soldat parlant français — pour moi, ce devait être un milicien — m'a demandé : « Qui est cette femme ? ». « C'est tata ». Il est descendu voir les officiers dans la décapotable qui nous suivait. Il y a eu un conciliabule avec d'autres ouvrières de la fabrique. Le milicien est revenu et m'a fait descendre. Après, tout ce dont je me souviens, c'est que je me suis retrouvé sous les tables entre les jupes des ouvrières, à manger des bonbons. »

Bouches cousues

Pourquoi a-t-il été libéré ? René Wucher l'ignore toujours. Peut-être parce qu'il n'était pas juif. « Mais, dit-il, à ma connaissance, parmi ceux qui ont été emmenés, il y en avait d'autres dans mon cas

René Wucher, plus tard, a rejoint son père à Murs. Pas pour longtemps. En août 1944, **Antoine, pris dans une rafle, a été fusillé. Les Résistants ont emmené René à Saint-Germain-les-Paroisses, où, à la fin de la guerre, une tante est venue le chercher.**

Lorsque quelques années furent passées, André, l'aîné, est revenu à Izieu. Il voulait savoir comment son père avait été arrêté, pourquoi René avait été mis en pension à Izieu et pourquoi on l'avait libéré. Mais, **au seul nom de Wucher, les bouches se sont closes.** René lui-même a retrouvé la cousine qui l'avait sauvé. Mais, pas plus que les autres, elle n'a voulu évoquer ces instants tragiques. René, a maintenant décidé de retourner à Izieu. Pour savoir enfin.

**José
BENJAMIN**

The One Who Was Released—René Wucher

Our investigation has established that all forty-four children deported after their arrest at Izieu were Jews.

René Wucher was not Jewish. When his cousin convinced the Gestapo of that fact, René was released. The Gestapo did not intend its criminal actions for non-Jewish children. It waged a total war against Jews only.

The article reproduced opposite appeared in the Paris daily newspaper *France-Soir* on February 23, 1983:

René Wucher lived through Barbie's raid at Izieu:

"Civilians in long coats took us away"

He was released shortly afterward. None of the 40 children or 10 adults arrested was ever seen again

On April 6, 1944, Barbie came to round up, at the children's home at Izieu, Ain, forty-one little Jewish residents, and the ten adults who made up the staff. They were never seen again. The sole exceptions were Dr. Reithman [sic] (30 at the time), who was able to jump out the window and hide, and little René Wucher, who was released several miles down the road, without knowing why.

René Wucher (47) today has two children and works at the Paris public transportation authority. The forces of domestic and economic necessity that reigned at the time had split his family in two. His mother and two of his brothers had stayed in the Paris metropolitan area. René had gone to meet up with his father, Antoine, and his older brother, André (10 at the time).

Antoine, a mechanic, was based several miles from Izieu in Murs, and worked most often on farms in the region. During the day, he made his rounds of the area by bicycle. René and André Wucher lacked for nothing, and, as well as they can remember, were happy. Such was the eight-year-old boy who, one fine day, found himself at the home in Izieu.

A piglet between his legs

"Even today," he recounts, "I still don't know why. I don't remember how long I was there. Undoubtedly several weeks, because my brother and my father came to visit me there. I have only vague memories of life at the home. They gave us a little bit of school, but not much. Most of the time, we were out playing in the yard."

That is all that an eight-year-old child was able to remember of a life which, up to that point, had been without real difficulties. But April 6, 1944, has left a deeper imprint on André's memory:

"Through the window, we saw the trucks arriving in the yard. There were few soldiers in them. There were mostly civilians, wearing long coats. They spread out all over, shouting. The staff of the home came to look for us, then everything happened very fast. The children and adults were separated, and I ended up in the back of a small truck, next to the fuel tank. I don't remember being hit. Outside, behind the vehicle I was in, I could catch a glimpse of a big convertible with four or five officers. The one next to the driver had a piglet between his legs. It's an image which has never left me. Inside the truck, we broke into song, I with all the rest. Perhaps, for the older ones, it was a way of making a statement. But for me, it was a camp song."

Two miles down the road, the convoy arrived at La Bruyère, at the intersection of the Izieu road.

René Wucher falls silent. He looks about the room, his eyes now brimming with tears. His voice quavering somewhat, he resumes:

"I've always been lucky, except at cards. That may be the day Lady Luck came into my life. At the crossroads, the convoy pulled up, because one of the vehicles had broken down. My truck was parked in front of a little candy factory where one of my cousins worked. When she caught sight of me, she almost fainted. A soldier who spoke French—as far as I can see, it must have been a member of the Milice—asked me: 'Who is that woman?' 'That's Auntie.' He went to see the officers in the convertible which was following us. There was hubbub among the other workers from the factory. The man from the Milice returned and had me get out. Afterward, all I remember is that I found myself under the table in the skirts of the workers, eating candy."

Sealed lips

Why was he released? René Wucher still doesn't know. Perhaps because he wasn't Jewish. "But," he says, "as far as I know, there were others in my situation among those who were taken away."

Later on, René Wucher rejoined his father in Murs. But not for long. In August 1944, Antoine, taken during a raid, was shot dead. Resistance members took René to Saint-Germain-les-Paroisses, where, at the end of the war, an aunt came to get him.

After a number of years had passed, André, his older brother, returned to Izieu. He wanted to know how his father had been arrested, why René had been placed in the home at Izieu, and why he had been released. But, at the mere mention of the name Wucher, people went dumb. René himself has located the cousin who rescued him. But she had no more desire than anyone else to call these tragic moments to mind. René has now decided to return to Izieu. To know at last.

[Picture caption:] He was eight years old in 1944. He was saved at the last moment.

Der Befehlshaber der Sicherheitspolizei und des SD
im Bereich des Militärbefehlshabers in Frankreich
Fernschreibstelle

Aufgenommen				Befördert				Raum für Eingangsstempel
Tag	Monat	Jahr	Zeit	Tag	Monat	Jahr	Zeit	
von – 6 AVRIL 1944 durch				an		durch		
				Verzögerungsvermerk				
FS.-Nr. 30420								
FS.-Annahme								
an:	Uhr. ab:			Uhr.				

Raum für Eingangsstempel:
– 7 APRIL 1944
33405
IV B
– 7 AVR 1944 14486/44

LYON NR. 5269 6.4.44 2010 UHR == FI =

= AN DEN BDS – ABTL. ROEM. 4 B – PARIS =

= BETR: JUEDISCHES KINDERHEIM IN IZIEU-AIN =

= VORG: OHNE ==

IN DEN HEUTIGEN MORGENSTUNDEN WURDE DAS JUEDISCHE

KINDERHEIM '' COLONIÉ ENFANT '' IN IZIEU-AIN AUSGEHOBEN.

INSGESAMT WURDEN 41 KINDER IM ALTER VON 3 BIS 13 JAHREN

FESTGENOMMEN. FERNER GELANG DIE FESTNAHME DES GESAMTEN

JUEDISCHEN PERSONALS , BESTEHEND AUS 10 KOEPFEN,

DAVON 5 FRAUEN. BARGELD ODER SONSTIGE VERMOEGENSWERTE

KONNTEN NICHT SICHERGESTELLT WERDEN ==

= DER ABTRANSPORT NACH DRANCY ERFOLGT AM 7.4.44 ==

DER KDR. DER SIPO UND DES SD LYON ROEM. 4 B 61/43

I. A. GEZ. BARBIE S.S-OSTUF==

[handschriftliche Notizen]

I Org — 580 — 100 000

THE IZIEU TELEX

At 8:10 P.M. on April 6, 1944, the evening of the Izieu raid, the following telex announcing the liquidation of the home for Jewish children at Izieu was sent by Klaus Barbie to the Commander of the Security Police and Security Service for France, marked to the attention of the Office for Jewish Affairs, known as Department IV B.*

Lyon No. 5,269 4/6/44 8:10 p.m. - FI
To the B.d.S. - Dept. IV B - Paris
Re: Jewish children's home in Izieu, Ain
Previous: None
This morning the Jewish children's home "colonie enfant" in Izieu, Ain, was cleaned out. In total 41 children aged 3 through 13 years were apprehended. In addition the arrest of the entire Jewish staff, 10 strong, including 5 women, was carried out. Neither cash nor other valuables could be secured. Transport to Drancy to follow on 4/7/44.
The commanding officer of the Sipo-SD Lyon
Dept. IV B 61/43
By order of, signed: Barbie SS Obersturmführer

There were in fact forty-four children. However, owing to their age and, most probably, their maturity, Arnold Hirsch (seventeen years old), Theodor Reis (sixteen), and Fritz Löbmann (fifteen) must have been considered staff and counted with the adults rather than the children.

The History of the Telex

This telex was presented by the French delegation at Nuremberg as documentary proof of the crimes committed by the Nazis against the Jews in France. It was retained by the International Military Tribunal as an Exhibit—that is, it was selected for possible use in the war crimes trials. It therefore received a classification number, RF 1235 (RF for République française, French Republic).

*B.d.S. is the abbreviation for Befehlshaber der Sicherheitspolizei und des Sicherheitsdienst, the head of the Sipo-SD in France. In the original version of Barbie's telex, reproduced opposite, "ABTL. [Abteilung, or department] ROEM. [Römisch, indicating Roman numeral] 4 B" denotes "Dept. IV. B," the Office for Jewish Affairs located in Paris. "DER KDR. DER SIPO UND DES SD LYON" refers to the regional commanding officer of the Sipo-SD based in Lyon (Dr. Werner Knab at the time). Barbie's position was head of Dept. IV of the Sipo-SD—the Gestapo; his rank, obersturmführer ("OSTUF" in the telex), was the SS equivalent of first lieutenant.

Opposite: The Izieu telex, signed by Barbie and sent from Lyon on April 6, 1944, at 8:10 P.M. The handwritten annotations at the bottom of the telex, added at the Gestapo's Office for Jewish Affairs in Paris, read:

1) Affair discussed in the presence of Dr. v.B. and Hauptsturmführer Brunner. Dr. v.B. stated that in such cases special measures regarding the lodging of children had been provided for by Obersturmführer Röthke. Hauptsturmführer Brunner replied that he had no knowledge of such instructions or plans, and that as a matter of principle he would not consent to such special measures. In these cases also he would proceed in the normal manner as regards deportation. For the time being I have made no decision in principle.
2) Obersturmführer Röthke for information and decision.

Dr. v.B. (von Behr), director of the Einsatzstab Rosenberg in Paris, supervised the confiscation of deported Jews' furniture and valuables. He committed suicide in 1945.

B o r d e r e a u.
-.-.-.-.-.-.-.-.-.-.-.-.-.

.1)	Table des noms		1 page	
2)	Doc. 23 - 24-12-41 - Télégramme du SS-Gruppenführer Müller au Chargé du Chef de la SP et du SD Dr. Knochen, Paris		3 feuilles	XXVI-5
.3)	" 24 - 4-2-42 - Lettre du SS-Sturmbannführer Hagen au Service IV J paris	1	"	XXVI-6
	11-11-41 - Lettre de "Otto et Hilde" adressée à Mme Anna Barbasz, Lisbonne	2	"	
4)	" 25 - 21-2-42 - Lettre du Frontstalag 122 Compiègne au Militärbefehlshaber Paris	2	"	
	18-2-42 - Rapport du Médecin du camp	1	"	
5)	" 27 - 9-5-42 - Télégramme de Bordeaux au Service IV J Paris (signé Doberschütz)	2	"	XXVI-20
6)	" 28 - 14-5-42 - Lettre du Dr. Schmidt au Serv. IV J	1	"	XXVI-22
7)	" 29 - 8-7-42 - Note de Dannecker adressée à Lischka	4	"	XXVI-55
8)	" 30 - 15-7-42 - Note de Röthke à Dannecker	2	"	XXVI-45
9)	" 31 - 21-7-42 - Note de Dannecker	2	"	XXVI-4?
1o)	" 32 - 4-8-42 - Note du SS-Sturmbannführer Hagen adressée à Heinrichsohn et Röthke	2	"	
11)	" 33 - 27-8-42 - Note de SS-Unterscharführer Heinrichsohn au Dr. Knochen	2	"	
12)	" 34 - 1-9-42 - Note de SS-Untersturmführer Ahnert à Lischka et au Dr. Knochen	3	"	
13)	" 35 - 12-9-42 - Note de Röthke à Knochen et Lischka	5	"	XX?-?3
14)	" 36 - 23-9-42 - Telegramme de Roethke au RSHA, Berlin	2	"	XXVI-?4
15)	" 37 - 25-9-42 - Télégramme du Dr. Knochen au RSHA, IV B 4, Berlin	2	"	XXVI-1??
16)	" 38 - 14-1-43 - Lettre du Chef de la SP et du SD,Berlin adressée à tous les services du SD et SP	1	"	VII-3
	6-1-43 - Instructions pour les exécutions capitales	5	"	
17)	" 39 - 3o-3-43 - Lettre du Befehlshaber de la Police d'ordre au BdS, Paris	1	"	
	24-3-43 - Rapport	4	"	
	26-3-43 - Rapport	2	"	
	27-3-43 - Conclusion	1	"	

50 feuilles./...

- 2 -

18)	Doc. 4o - 15-8-43 - Note de Röthke à Knochen		4 feuilles	
	12-4-43 - Note de Hagen au BdS		1 "	
	avec annexe		1 "	
	21-5-43 - Réponse		2 "	
19)	" 41 - 21-7-43 - Note de SS-Obersturmführer Röthke		2 "	
2o)	" 42 - 3-12-43- Rapport de F. Köhnlein de la Schutzpolizei à Röthke		1 "	
21)	" 43 - 6-4-44 - Télégramme de SS-Obersturmführer Bartie (Lyon) au BdS, Paris		1 "	

Transport: 5o   "

Total: 62 feuilles

Memo listing documents borrowed by the
French delegation to the Nuremberg trials.

The original of the telex came from the archives of the Office for Jewish Affairs of the Gestapo in France. These archives had been taken over upon the liberation of Paris by the CDJC (Centre de Documentation Juive Contemporaine, or Jewish Contemporary Documentation Center), which in 1943 had been started in secret at Grenoble by Isaac Schneerson, whose aim was to gather documentary proof of the persecution suffered by the Jews in France during the war. The French delegation had addressed itself to the CDJC in 1945 in order to obtain the documents it needed to demonstrate the precise nature, scope, and severity of the anti-Jewish persecutions in France.

On January 23, 1946, the delegation borrowed twenty-five documents, which would later become Exhibits. Several days later, it borrowed a second series of twenty-two, which are listed in the memorandum reproduced opposite; the Barbie telex is number twenty-one on the list.

At Nuremberg, the procedure was in general as follows: the staff charged with the preparation of the trials made a photostat of the original document; this photocopy was immediately authenticated and the original returned to the power that had submitted it—in the case of Barbie's telex, France, as represented by the French delegation to the trials.

Unfortunately, however, a number of the forty-seven original documents—which had been photocopied for safety's sake by the CDJC before it had turned them over to the French delegation—were never returned to the CDJC. We believed this to be the case with Barbie's telex, as we had only the photocopy in our possession when we established a dossier on Barbie and began our investigation in 1971.

In October 1982, when we went to the Elysée Palace, the official residence of the president of France, to discuss the conditions of Barbie's possible return to France, we remarked upon the necessity of finding the original of this telex, which we could not locate at all at the CDJC. We received authorization to look through the files of the ministries of justice and foreign affairs, within whose jurisdiction the Nuremberg trials had fallen, as well as through France's national archives, where a portion of the French delegation's papers might have been stored.

Our search was to no avail. We addressed ourselves to the International Court of Justice in The Hague, which we knew had collected a large part of the archives from the Nuremberg trials. In his reply, the clerk of the court addressed an essential point: the authenticated copy of the Barbie telex placed in exhibit at Nuremberg was to be found under the number H-4826 in the archives of the Nuremberg International Military Tribunal, which had been placed in storage at the International Court of Justice.

The photocopy in The Hague matched perfectly that at the CDJC in Paris. In view of the rigor of the procedures followed, and of the exact conformity of the two photocopies, both of which had been authenticated from the original telex, there could be no doubt as to the existence and authenticity of the original. In addition, another authenticated copy of the telex can be found in Washington, D.C., where photostated copies of the exhibits introduced in Nuremberg by the British, French, and Russian prosecutors, as well as the originals of the United States exhibits, are in the custody of the National Archives.

Barbie's impudent challenge to the telex's authenticity led us to resume our investigation. We thought that perhaps a member of the French delegation at Nuremberg had held on to documents covering Jewish matters, or had placed them in an inappropriate archival collection where they might never be located. We were left with only one hypothesis that allowed us even a slim chance of success: the possibility that the telex had been engulfed in the mountains of files generated in the course of the CDJC's business and relegated to the storerooms of that worthy institution.

As soon as I received authorization, I began a search of the vaults, assisted by the CDJC's archivist. We had the joy of uncovering the telex in a folder containing material relating to the trial of Otto Abetz, the German ambassador in Paris. It is likely that a CDJC staff member, having an appointment with the examining magistrate in the Abetz case, had brought with him the original of the Barbie telex—returned to the CDJC by the French delegation in 1946—to show what had befallen the Jews during Abetz's term as ambassador. The magistrate would not have kept the document in his possession, there being no direct connection between the activities of Abetz in 1944 and this initiative of the Lyon Gestapo, so the CDJC staff member must then have brought the folder back to the center, omitting to return the telex to the place where it had been filed alongside the photocopy.

Found through our efforts, the original of the telex—along with other original documents signed by Barbie that the CDJC had in its possession—quickly made its way into the hands of the examining magistrate in Lyon charged with the Barbie case. The CDJC and the magistrate have taken every precaution to ensure that all the documents will be returned to the center at the conclusion of the legal proceedings against Barbie.

Letter from the court clerk of the International Court of Justice to Serge Klarsfeld regarding the original of the Barbie telex:

March 14, 1983

Maître,

In response to your letter of March 7, 1983, I have the honor of informing you that the archives of the International Military Tribunal at Nuremberg, which have been entrusted to the International Court of Justice, contain only those documents retained as Exhibits by the International Military Tribunal. They represent, therefore, only a portion of those documents that were in the possession of the prosecution in the course of the trial of the major war criminals. Sometimes the document on file with the Court is only a photocopy of the original, and no indication has been given as to the final destination of that original. Such is the case, among others, of the document of April 6, 1944, mentioned by you. Exhibit RF 1235, registered at the Court under the number H-4826, is only a photocopy. It matches precisely the photocopy enclosed with your letter, carries a registration on the back, and is preceded by a mimeographed document. I enclose with this letter photocopies of all of these documents. I enclose as well a photocopy of Exhibit RF 1051, which is preceded by the original report, referred to in the above-mentioned mimeographed document.

I do not believe, in these circumstances, that you will judge it necessary to come next March 17 to consult the archives at the Court. If that be nevertheless the case, you will be welcome, and I would kindly ask you to address yourself directly to Mr. Witteveen, librarian of the Court, who will guide you in your researches.

Sincerely,

The Clerk of the Court

COUR INTERNATIONALE DE JUSTICE   INTERNATIONAL COURT OF JUSTICE

PALAIS DE LA PAIX 2517 KJ LA HAYE PAYS-BAS   PEACE PALACE 2517 KJ THE HAGUE NETHERLANDS
TÉLÉPHONE: (070) 92 44 41 TÉLEX: 32323   TELEPHONE: (070) 92 44 41 TELEX: 32323
TÉLÉGR.: INTERCOURT LAHAYE   CABLES: INTERCOURT THEHAGUE

69645   Le 14 mars 1983

Maître,

En réponse à votre lettre du 7 mars 1983, j'ai l'honneur de vous faire connaître que les archives du Tribunal militaire international de Nuremberg déposées auprès de la Cour internationale de Justice contiennent uniquement les documents retenus comme exhibits par le Tribunal militaire international. Ils ne correspondent donc qu'à une partie des documents qui étaient en la possession de l'accusation au cours du procès des grands criminels de guerre. Parfois le document déposé à la Cour n'est qu'une photocopie de l'original et aucune indication n'est donnée quant à la destination définitive de l'original. Tel est le cas notamment pour la pièce du 6 avril 1944 par vous mentionnée. L'exhibit RF 1235 enregistré à la Cour sous la côte H-4826 n'est qu'une photocopie. Elle correspond exactement à la photocopie jointe à votre lettre, elle porte au verso un enregistrement et elle est précédée d'un document polycopié. Je joins à la présente lettre des photocopies de l'ensemble de ces pièces. J'y joins aussi une photocopie de l'exhibit RF 1051, lequel est précédé du procès-verbal original mentionné dans le document polycopié susindiqué.

Je ne pense pas que, dans ces conditions, vous jugerez nécessaire de venir consulter le 17 mars prochain les archives déposées auprès de la Cour. Si tel était cependant le cas, vous seriez le bienvenu et je vous demanderai de bien vouloir vous adresser directement à M. Witteveen, bibliothécaire de la Cour, qui vous guiderait dans vos recherches.

Veuillez agréer, Maître, l'assurance de ma considération distinguée.

Le Greffier de la Cour

Santiago Torres Bernárdez

Maître Klarsfeld
Avocat à la Cour
32 rue de la Boétie
75008 Paris
France

Opposite: Article from the Paris newspaper *Journal du Dimanche*, which appeared in 1984. The text of the telex differs here from that on page 95, as it has been retranslated from the French translation that was presented to the article's readers.

Found by attorney Klarsfeld, it proves that the Nazi had 41 Jewish children deported

It's the telex that indicts Barbie

Mr. Vergès loses a point. The centerpiece of the Barbie file has been located by his adversary, Mr. Klarsfeld, in the archives of the Jewish Contemporary Documentation Center in Paris.

The object in question is a telex, which had been placed among tons of yellowing papers in the wrong file: that of Germany's wartime ambassador to Paris, Otto Abetz.

This document is essential, for, according to the prosecution, it proves that Klaus Barbie has indeed incurred the guilt of a crime against humanity—a crime for which there is no statute of limitation—in participating in the deportation of Jewish children to Auschwitz. The following is a translation of the telegram reproduced above, dispatched from Lyon on April 6, 1944, at 8:10 P.M., and registered the same evening at the Gestapo in Paris:

"This morning a stop was put to the activities of

Retrouvé par Mᵉ Klarsfeld, il prouve que le nazi a fait déporter 41 enfants juifs

C'est le télex qui accuse Barbie

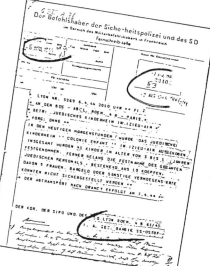

Mᵉ Vergès perd un point. La pièce maîtresse du dossier Barbie vient d'être retrouvée par son adversaire, Mᵉ Klarsfeld, dans les archives du Centre de documentation juive contemporaine, à Paris.

Il s'agit d'un télex égaré dans un autre dossier, celui de l'ambassadeur allemand à Paris pendant la guerre, Otto Abetz, parmi des tonnes de papiers jaunis.

Ce document est essentiel car, d'après l'accusation, il démontre que Klaus Barbie s'est bien rendu coupable de crime contre l'humanité — imprescriptible — en participant à la déportation d'enfants juifs vers Auschwitz. Voici la traduction du texte du télégramme expédié de Lyon le 6 avril 1944, à 20 h 10, et enregistré le même soir à la Gestapo de Paris, et que nous reproduisons ci-joint.

« Il a été mis fin ce matin aux activités du foyer d'enfants juifs "colonie enfant" d'Izieu-Ain. Au total quarante et un enfants âgés de trois à treize ans ont été arrêtés. De plus l'ensemble du personnel juif, soit dix têtes dont cinq femmes, a également été arrêté. Il n'a été trouvé ni argent liquide, ni autres objets de valeur. Le transport vers Drancy aura lieu le 7 avril 1944. »

Et c'est signé : « Le commandeur du Sipo (police de sécurité et du SD (service de renseignement), Lyon IV B 61/43, par ordre lieutenant SS Barbie. »

Ce télex, dont la justice ne possédait jusqu'à présent qu'une copie certifiée conforme à l'original, était toujours contesté par Barbie. Pour lui ce document est un faux, en ce moins. Il défait : « Montrez-moi donc l'original ! » Et il avait porté plainte.

Or l'original, on ne le trouvait ni dans les archives de la Cour internationale de La Haye — gardienne des pièces à conviction du procès des grands chefs nazis à Nuremberg —, ni dans les papiers de la justice militaire. Aujourd'hui Mᵉ Klarsfeld exhibe l'original. Réaction de Mᵉ Vergès : « Rien ne prouve qu'il est authentique ! »

Des tampons français

Alors les experts vont devoir examiner ce document à la loupe. Il y a en tout cas deux questions auxquelles ils ne pourront pas répondre :

1. — Pourquoi Barbie a signé I.A. (Im Auftrag), c'est-à-dire « par ordre », alors que l'affaire relevait, prétend Barbie, d'un subalterne, le SS Wenzel ou son collègue Bartelmus ?

2. — Pourquoi deux des trois tampons dateurs apposés à la réception du télétype à Paris sont-ils des tampons français ? L'un indique 6 avril, en toutes lettres, l'autre 7 avr et non pas April, comme il est écrit sur le troisième, en haut à droite.

Est-ce dire que les Allemands manquaient de cachet ?

Pour mettre un terme à cette polémique, Serge Klarsfeld a versé au dossier d'instruction d'autres télégrammes du même type, envoyés le même jour par d'autres bureaux régionaux de la Gestapo : ils comportent les mêmes « erreurs », I.A. et les dates en français.

En définitive, si ce document est faux, c'est qu'il a été fabriqué avant 1946, car il avait déjà été produit à Nuremberg... il y a trente-sept ans. Et à cette époque Klaus Barbie était un SS insignifiant parmi les grands criminels de guerre. Il n'était que le 239ᵉ de la liste. Personne ne parlait encore de lui et pour cause... les services secrets américains allaient l'utiliser comme agent spécial.

LADISLAS DE HOYOS

---

the home for Jewish children 'colonie enfant' of Izieu, Ain. Forty-one children aged from three to thirteen years were arrested. In addition the entire Jewish staff, ten strong including five women, was arrested as well. Neither cash nor other valuables were found. Transport to Drancy will take place April 7, 1944."

And it is signed: "The commanding officer of the Sipo (security police) and SD (intelligence service), Lyon IV B 61/43, by order SS lieutenant Barbie."

This telex, of which the prosecution had, up to now, only a copy certified as matching the original, was always disputed by Barbie. According to him, the document is nothing less than a forgery. He challenged: "Bring on the original!" And he filed a complaint.

Now, as to the original, it was not to be found, neither in the archives of the International Court in The Hague—keeper of the evidence that convicted the big Nazi chiefs at the Nuremberg trials—nor in the papers of the military court. Today Mr. Klarsfeld displays the original. Mr. Vergès's reaction: "Nothing proves that it's authentic!"

French Stamps

Thus, the experts are going to have to put this document under a microscope. There are, in any event, two questions they will not be able to answer:

1) Why did Barbie sign I.A. (Im Auftrage), that is to say, "by order of," while the deed rests— Barbie claims—with a subordinate, SS man Wentzel or his colleague Bartelmus?

2) Why are two of the three date stamps, applied upon receipt of the teletyped message in Paris, in French? One indicates "6 avril," spelled out, the other "7 avr" and not "April," as written on the third, in the upper right.

Is it, so to speak, that the Germans could make no impression on their own?

To put an end to these polemics, Serge Klarsfeld has contributed to the investigation of the case other telegrams of the same type, sent the same day by other regional bureaus of the Gestapo: they include the same "errors": I.A., and dates in French.

If this document ultimately proves false, then the fact is that it was forged before 1946, because it was brought forth at Nuremberg...thirty-seven years ago. And at that time, Klaus Barbie was, amid the major war criminals, an insignificant member of the SS. He was only 239th on the list. No one yet talked about him, and for a very good reason...the American Secret Services were going to use him as a special agent.

The Date Stamps

Barbie's defense attorneys claimed astonishment that only French-language date stamps appear on the telex. However, it must be noted that the date stamps are not only in French—there are two in French and one in German. This was the customary procedure from at least 1942 on, as dozens of similar telexes preserved by the CDJC attest.

For example, an original telex from Marseilles signed "Muehler" (page 102) and sent on April 6, 1944, at 8:20 P.M. (20 20) —ten minutes after Barbie's telex left Lyon (20 10 UHR)— shows the same date stamps in the same places as on the Barbie telex. Two are in French: one at the upper left, reading 6 AVRIL 1944, the other at the upper right, reading 7 AVR 1944. The second French stamp is followed by the reference 14486/44 on the Lyon telex, which was marked by hand 9:25 P.M (21 25) on arrival in Paris, and by the reference 14488/44 on the Marseilles telex, marked 10:00 P.M. (22 00) when it arrived.

The German date stamp 7 APRIL 1944 is to be found in a rectangle at the upper right, just above the second French date stamp. It is followed by the number 33405 on the Lyon telex, and 33421 on the Marseilles telex. At the upper left, the Lyon telex carries the number 30420; the slightly later Marseilles telex carries the number 30448.

The first French date stamp indicates the date the telex was dispatched, while the German date stamp gives the date it was registered by the Sipo-SD's General Service, which was responsible for distributing mail and messages. The second French date stamp undoubtedly indicates the date on which the telex was registered by the office to which it was addressed.

The Signature

The signature "Barbie" is preceded by the abbreviation I.A.—im Auftrage, by order. This signifies simply that the party in question is signing within the normal exercise of his functions. Had Barbie signed I.V.—in Vertretung, in the name—that would indicate that he was signing for a superior who would normally be qualified to sign, but was absent.

Heinrich Müller, head of the Gestapo, and Adolf Eichmann, head of the Gestapo's anti-Jewish section, often preceded their signatures with the abbreviation I.A. (Compare document page 104, signed I.A. Eichmann; this document also carries date stamps as described above.)

On the other hand, the commander of the Sipo-SD in a given region signed his name only, never placing before it the abbreviation I.A. or I.V. This is the case for the April 6, 1944, telex from Marseilles signed by Muehler, and for a September 14, 1943, telex from Lyon signed by Dr. Knab (page 103).

The Backing Paper

The strips of telex bearing Barbie's message are pasted onto a telex form printed on the back of a map. This is not an English map, as Barbie's defense claims; rather, the communications office of the B.d.S., which received the telex, cut down and used as printing stock maps of Great Britain printed by the Germans. It was standard practice in 1944 to use these maps as an economy measure. They had doubtless been printed in 1940, when an invasion of England appeared in the offing, but had been rendered useless by the course of military events. The April 6, 1944, telex from Marseilles is pasted onto another piece of the same map. The same is true for the telex of April 22, 1944, from Marseilles, signed I.A. Bauer; for the telex of April 4, 1944, from Marseilles, whose signature, likely to have been I.A. Bauer, has come off; for the telex of May 16, 1944, from Nice, signed by the head of the local Sipo-SD, Dr. Keil; and for other German telexes not reproduced here. Moreover, the back of the April 4, 1944, telex shows clearly that the map was printed by the Germans, as the margin contains both heading and printed notations in German.

In addition, all of the telexes bear the two French date stamps, plus the single German date stamp inscribed in the rectangle at the upper right. And the reference numbers correspond in all cases to the order in which the telexes were received.

Der Befehlshaber der Sicherheitspolizei und des S D
im Bereich des Militärbefehlshabers in Frankreich
Fernschreibstelle

Aufgenommen				Befördert				Raum für Eingangsstempel
Tag	Monat	Jahr	Zeit	Tag	Monat	Jahr	Zeit	
von	-6 AVRIL 1944	durch		an	durch			-7 Avril 1944
								33405
FS.-Nr.	3049,0		Verzögerungsvermerk					IV B
								-7 AVR 1944 /4486/44
	FS.-Annahme							
an:		Uhr. ab:			Uhr.			

= LYON NR. 5269 6.4.44 2010 UHR == FI. =

XLVI-1-7

Der Befehlshaber der Sicherheitspolizei und des S D
im Bereich des Militärbefehlshabers in Frankreich
Fernschreibstelle

Aufgenommen				Befördert				Raum für Eingangsstempel
Tag	Monat	Jahr	Zeit	Tag	Monat	Jahr	Zeit	
von	6 AVRIL 19..	durch		an	durch			-7 Avril 1944
								33421
FS.-Nr.	30448		Verzögerungsvermerk					IV B4
	FS.-Annahme							AVR 1944 /4488/44
an:		Uhr. ab:			Uhr.			

| — MARSEILLE — 3737 — 6.4.44 — 2020 — ALB •

Top: Heading of telex sent from Lyon on April
6, 1944 (6.4.44), at 8:10 P.M. (2010). Above:
Heading of telex sent from Marseilles on April
6, 1944 (6.4.44), at 8:20 P.M. (2020).

Der Befehlshaber der Sicherheitspolizei und des S D
im Bereich des Militärbefehlshabers in Frankreich
Fernschreibstelle

Aufgenommen				Befördert				Raum für Eingangsstempel
Tag	Monat	Jahr	Zeit	Tag	Monat	Jahr	Zeit	
von – 6 AVRIL 19..				an		durch		– 7 APR 1944
		durch						33421
FS.-Nr. 30448			Verzögerungsvermerk					IV 34
								AVR 1944 /4488/44
FS.-Annahme								
an:		Uhr. ab:		Uhr.				

```
- MARSEILLE - 3737 - 6.4.44 - 2020 - ALB -
AN DEN BDS - ROEM. 4 B - P A R I S .-
BETR: DIE JUDEN '' JONNY'' UND ELSA    K A G A N.-
VORG: DORT. SCHR. VOM 21.3.44 ROEM. 4 B 4 - SA 284 ROE/ NE.
- DAS IM VORGANG GENANNTE KABARETT '' BIARRITZ'' WAR BEREITS
VON DER HIES. DIENSTSTELLE GESCHLOSSEN WORDEN. U. A.
WURDEN FESTGENOMMEN DIE BESITZERIN K R I E F MIT ZWEI
TOECHTERN SOWIE DER BARMAN L I P S C H I T Z .-
BEI '' JONNY'' HANDELT ES SICH UM EINEN NICHTJUDEN NAMENS
S A N I T R I O .- UEBER DIE ELSA   K A G A N KONNTE NICHTS
IN ERFAHRUNG  GEBRACHT WERDEN.-
ZWECKS WEITERER ERMITTLUNGEN WIRD VORGANG AN DIE SIPO - SD
- AUSSENDIENSTSTELLE AVIGNNON WEITERGELEITET.-
DIE FESTGENOMMENEN JUDEN GELANGEN DEMNAECHST   ZUM ABSCHUB
IN DAS JUDENLAGER  DRANCY.-

PO - SD KDO - MARSEILLL - ROEM. 4 B - PA  3661/44   BA - ELS.
- DER KDR. M U E H L E R  - SS STBAF+ +
```

BdS. I Org - 58° - 190 000

Opposite: Full text of telex sent from Marseilles on April 6, 1944, at 8:20 P.M.:

Marseilles - 3737 - 4/6/44 - 8:20 P.M. - ALB - To the B.d.S. - IV B - Paris. -

Re: The Jews "Jonny" and Elsa Kagan.
Previous: Memo from there of 3/21/44 IV B 4 - SA 284 Röthke/NE.

The cabaret "Biarritz" named in previous had already been closed down by the bureau here. Among others, the proprietress Krief and two daughters, as well as the bartender Lipschitz were arrested. The "Jonny" in question is a non-Jew by the name of Sanitrio. Nothing could be learned about Elsa Kagan. Previous will be forwarded to the Sipo-SD field post in Avignon for further inquiry. The arrested Jews will be transported soon to the Drancy camp for Jews.

Sipo-SD Detachment - Marseilles - IV B - FA 3661/44 BA - ELS.
The Commanding Officer Muehler - SS Sturmbannführer

Right: A telex sent from Lyon on September 14, 1943, by Dr. Werner Knab, the commanding officer of the Sipo-SD for the Lyon region. Only the commanding officer could sign without placing I.A. or I.V. before his name.

Einsatzkommando Lyon, 6662. 9/14/43. 3:15 A.M.
WEL. - - To B.d.S. - IV B. - Paris. -
Secret. -

Re: Italian occupation troops' friendly behavior toward Jews.
Previous: None.

As reliably reported here, the commanders of the Italian detachments in France on September 5 or 6, 1943, received an order to issue on demand to all Jews residing in the territory under their command permits giving the Jews the possibility of freely changing their domicile within the zone in France occupied by Italian troops. The permits were for the period up to the evening of 9/9/43. Numerous Jews have fled in the past few days from the hitherto Italian-occupied departments in the hope that they will still be able to escape from there to Italy and thus elude the grasp of the Germans. Through the speedy blockade of the German-French borders only relatively few Jews should succeed in crossing the border. Please take note. Further reports on the treatment of the Jews by the Italian occupation authorities in France will follow shortly.

Einsatzkommando Lyon - VI N 1 - 145-MO/HT.
Signed Dr. Knab, Obersturmbannführer

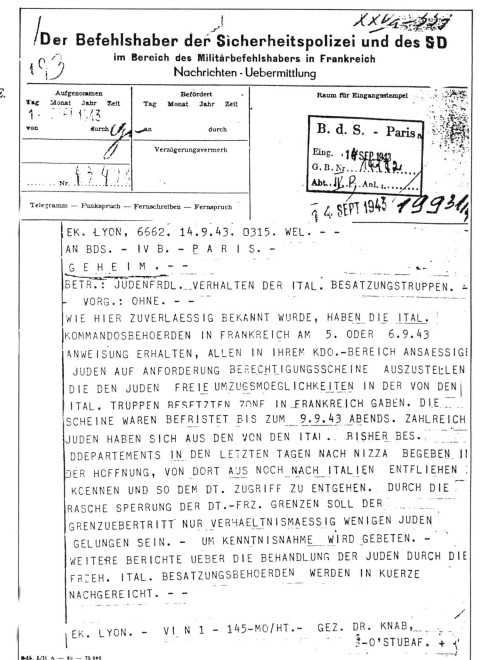

Der Befehlshaber der Sicherheitspolizei und des SD
im Bereich des Militärbefehlshabers in Frankreich
Nachrichten-Übermittlung

+B L I T Z- BERLIN NUE 7852 27.1.44 NA == GEHEIM ==
AN ALLE STAPO(LEIT)STELLEN- ALLE BEFEHLSHABER DER
SICHERHEITSPOLIZEI UND DES SD- AN DEN BEAUFTR. D. SIPO U.D.
SD IN BRUESSEL-
NACHRICHTLICH A) AN DIE HOEHEREN SS- U. POLIZEIFUEHRER.
B) AN DIE INSP. D. SICHERHEITSPOLIZEI UND DES SD. ==
BETR.: JUDEN ARGENTINISCHER STAATSANGEHOERIGKEIT. ==
BEZUG: O. ==
SAEMTLICHE JUDEN UND JUEDINNEN ARGENTINISCHER
STAATSANGEHOERIGKEIT SIND S O F O R T FESTZUNEHMEN.--
DIESE JUDEN SIND UMGEHENDST UNTER BEWACHUNG DEM
AUFENTHALTSLAGER BERGEN-BELSEN, CELLE BEI HANNOVER
ZUZUFUEHREN UND DORT DEM MIT DEN SICHERHEITSPOLIZEILICHEN
AUFGABEN BEAUFTRAGTEN SS-HAUPTSTURMFUEHRER DR. SEIDL ZU
UEBERGEBEN.- DAS VERMOEGEN DER FESTGENOMMENEN IST
SICHERZUSTELLEN. NACH VOLLZUGSMELDUNG ERFOLGEN WEITERE
WEISUNGEN.-
ZUSATZ FUER BDS. DEN HAAG.- SAEMTLICHE BISHER ENTSTANDENEN
VORGAENGE SIND ALS UEBERHOLT ANZUSEHEN. ===

= RSHA ROEM 4 B 4- I.A. GEZ. EICHMANN SS-O'STUBAF +

Above: A telex signed by Adolf Eichmann, who often placed I.A. before his signature:

Urgent - Berlin Nue 7852 1/27/44 NA = Secret = To all Gestapo Headquarters - all B.d.S. - to the delegate of the Sipo-SD in Brussels -

For informational purposes a) to the Higher SS and Police Leaders. b) to the Inspectors of the Sipo-SD-

Re : Jews of Argentine nationality
Reference: None

All Jews and Jewesses of Argentine nationality are to be arrested immediately. These Jews are to be transported under guard with the greatest dispatch to the residence camp Bergen-Belsen, Celle near Hanover, and to be handed over there to SS Hauptsturmführer Dr. Seidl, who is charged with the duties of the Sipo. The property of those arrested is to be secured. Further instructions will follow upon notice of execution.

Postscript for B.d.S. The Hague. - All hitherto arising procedures are to be considered superseded.

RSHA IV B 4- by order signed Eichmann SS Obersturmbannführer

Opposite, above left: The reverse of the Marseilles telex of April 6, 1944. Opposite, above right: The reverse of Barbie's telex of April 6, 1944, from Lyon. Opposite, below: Telex signed I.A. Bauer, sent on April 22, 1944, from Marseilles; on its reverse, part of a map of England.

SD - Marseilles No. 4571 4/22/44 2:45 P.M. = SR To the B.d.S. - IV B. - Paris. -
Re: Andre Ausch, born 7/13/90 in Tolna and wife Marguerite, née Sandor, born 9/15/86 in Budapest.- Previous: Memos from there of 2/8/44 and 3/16/44 IV F 4 and B.d.S. memo of 4/11/44. - IV B. 4.-

The above had already been arrested on 10/10/43 and were transported on 10/13/43 to the Drancy camp for Jews.

The Commander of Sipo-SD Marseilles IV B PA 3872/44
by order signed Bauer SS Hauptscharführer

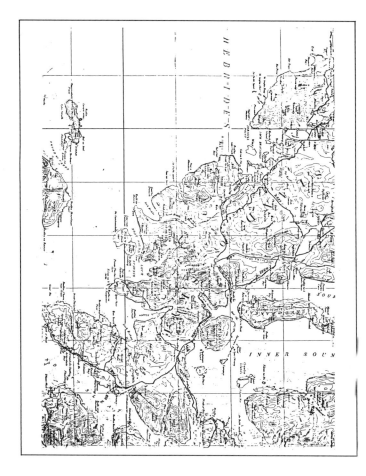

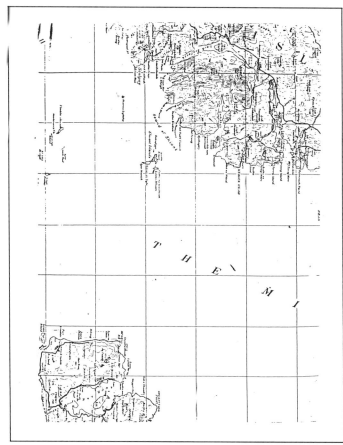

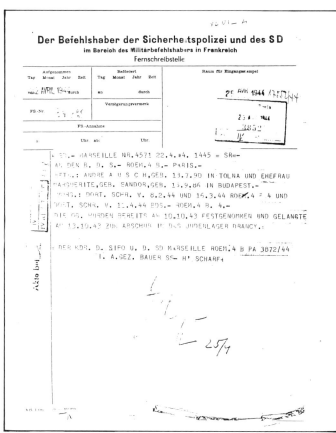

Der Befehlshaber der Sicherheitspolizei und des SD
im Bereich des Militärbefehlshabers in Frankreich
Fernschreibstelle

Aufgenommen				Befördert				Raum für Eingangsstempel
Tag	Monat	Jahr	Zeit	Tag	Monat	Jahr	Zeit	
von 2	AVRIL	194	durch	an			durch	25 AVRIL 1944
				Verzögerungsvermerk				
FS-Nr.								
	FS-Annahme							
a.		Uhr. ab:		Uhr.				

SD.- MARSEILLE NR.4571 22.4.44. 1445 = SR=-
AN DEN B. D. S. - ROEM.4 B.- PARIS.-
BETR.: ANDRE A U S C H,GEB. 13.7.90 IN TOLNA UND EHEFRAU
MARGUERITE,GEB. SANDOR,GEB. 13.9.86 IN BUDAPEST.-
BEZG.: DORT. SCHR. V. 8.2.44 UND 14.3.44 ROEM.4 B 4 UND
DORT. SCHR. V. 11.4.44 EDS.- ROEM.4 B. 4.-
DIE GG. WURDEN BEREITS AM 10.10.43 FESTGENOMMEN UND GELANGTE
AM 13.10.43 ZUM ABSCHUB IN DAS JUDENLAGER DRANCY.-

DER KDR. D. SIPO U. D. SD MARSEILLE ROEM.4 B PA 3872/44
I. A.GEZ. BAUER SS- H' SCHARF-

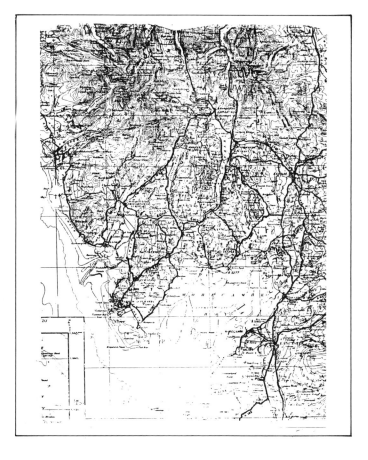

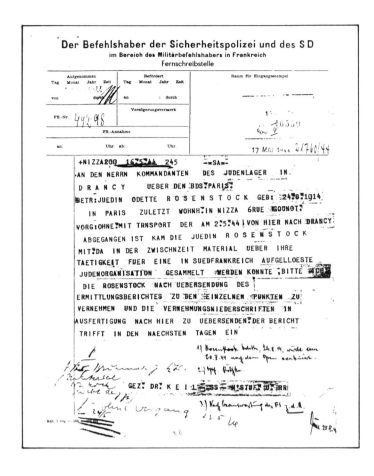

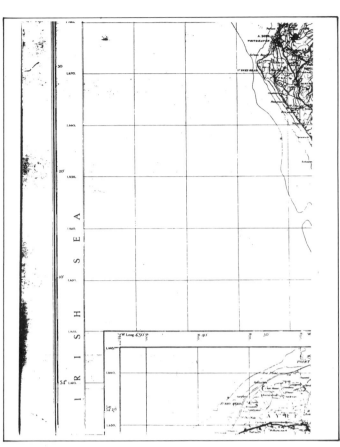

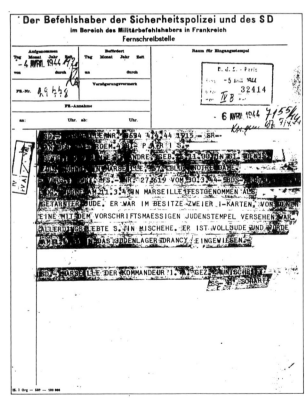

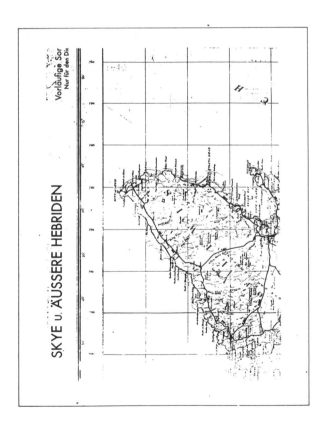

Top, left and right: Telex signed by the regional Sipo-SD head at Nice and sent on May 16, 1944; on the reverse, still another map of Great Britain. Above, left and right: Telex sent April 4, 1944, from Marseilles. The German-language titles on the border of the reverse of this telex establish beyond doubt that, for this entire series of telexes, the maps used for backing were German.

For complete English translations of these documents, see page 132.

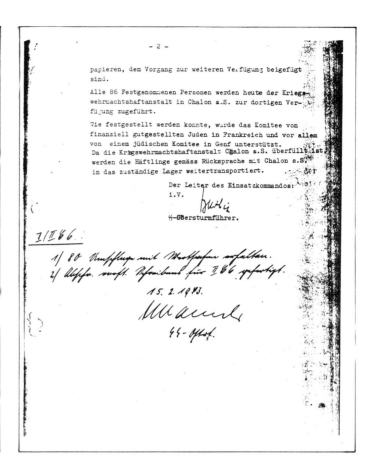

Sicherheitspolizei (SD)   Lyon, den 11.2.1943
Einsatzkommando L y o n

An den

Befehlshaber der Sicherheitspolizei und des SD
im Bereich des Militärbefehlshabers in Frankreich

P a r i s   IV F.

Betr.: Aushebung des jüdischen Komitees "Union General
des Israélites de France" (U.G.I.F.) Lyon.
Vorg.: Ohne.
Anlg.: 86 Festnahme- und Einlieferungsanzeichen je doppelt,
80 Briefumschläge mit Ausweispapieren und Wertgegenständen und eine Zusammenstellung (doppelt).

Der hiesigen Dienststelle wurde bekannt, dass sich in
Lyon, 12 rue St. Catherine, ein jüdisches Komitee befindet,
welches Emigranten unterstützt und Juden, die von Frankreich nach der Schweiz flüchten wollen, bei den Vorbe-
reitungen zum illegalen Grenzübertritt behilflich ist.
Am 9.2.43 wurde eine Aktion zur Aushebung des Komitees
durchgeführt. Beim Zugriff befanden sich bereits über 30
Juden in den Büroräumen. Alle Personen wurden zunächst festgenommen. Im Laufe einer weiteren Stunde erschienen noch
mehrere Juden und es konnten insgesamt 86 Personen festgenommen werden. Alle Festgenommenen wurden in einem Raum
zusammen untergebracht und, bevor die einzelnen Durch-
suchungen vorgenommen werden konnten, haben die meisten
Juden ihre falschen Identitätskarten und Ausweispapiere
vernichtet. Die meisten dieser Juden hatten die Absicht, in
nächster Zeit von hier aus nach der Schweiz zu flüchten.
Bei der Durchsuchung der Büroräume wurden eine grössere
Anzahl Wertgegenstände, ausländische Zahlungsmittel usw.
vorgefunden, deren Eigentümer sind bekannt sind. Ein Teil
der Eigentümer dürfte bereits nach der Schweiz geflüchtet
sein. Diese Wertgegenstände wurden beschlagnahmt und sind
im besonderen Umschlag beigefügt (siehe anhängende Auf-
stellung). Bei der Durchsuchung der einzelnen Personen
wurden weitere Wertgegenstände und Zahlungsmittel vorgefunden, die in einzelnen Umschlägen, zusammen mit den Ausweis-

- 2 -

papieren, dem Vorgang zur weiteren Verfügung beigefügt
sind.

Alle 86 Festgenommenen Personen werden heute der Kriegswehrmachtshaftanstalt in Chalon s.S. zur dortigen Verfügung zugeführt.

Wie festgestellt werden konnte, wurde das Komitee von
finanziell gutgestellten Juden in Frankreich und vor allem
von einem jüdischen Komitee in Genf unterstützt.
Da die Kriegswehrmachtshaftanstalt Chalon s.S. überfüllt ist,
werden die Häftlinge gemäss Rücksprache mit Chalon s.S.
in das zuständige Lager weitertransportiert.

Der Leiter des Einsatzkommandos:
i.V.

#-Obersturmführer.

R.F. SS
Sicherheits-Dienst
Nachrichten-Uebermittlung

Nr. 7311

LYON BLITZ FS NR.598 11.2.43 1245 == PETR. ==
AN DEN B D S PARIS ZU HD. VON # STANDARTENFUEHRER
DR. K N O C H E N .
BETR.: KOMITEE ZUR UNTERSTUETZUNG VON EMIGRANTEN UND
MITTELLOSEN JUDEN .
VORG.: DORTIGES FS-VERFUEGUNG 7209 VOM 10. FEBR. 1943 .
DA DIE AKTION GEGEN DAS GENANNTE KOMITEE VON HIER AUS
DURCHGEFUEHRT WURDE, SIND DIE JUDEN SELBSTVERSTAENDLICH IN
DEUTSCHEN GEWAHRSAM GENOMMEN WORDEN . ES HANDELT SICH
UM 86 PERSONEN DIE HEUTE UEBER CHALON S.S. NACH DEM
ZUSTAENDIGEN LAGER UEBERSTELLT WERDEN .
DER LEITER DES EK LYON I.V. GEZ. BARBIE #-0' STUF .

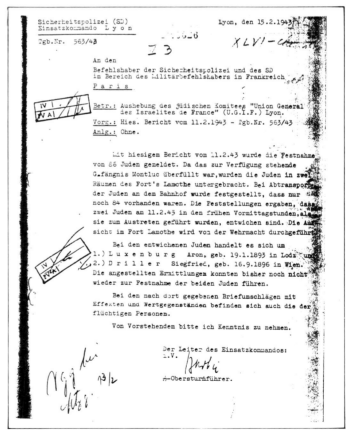

Sicherheitspolizei (SD)   Lyon, den 15.2.1943
Einsatzkommando L y o n
Tgb.Nr. 563/43

An den

Befehlshaber der Sicherheitspolizei und des SD
im Bereich des Militärbefehlshabers in Frankreich

P a r i s

Betr.: Aushebung des jüdischen Komitees "Union General
des Israelites de France" (U.G.I.F.) Lyon.
Vorg.: Hies. Bericht vom 11.2.1943 - Tgb.Nr. 563/43
Anlg.: Ohne.

Mit hiesigem Bericht vom 11.2.43 wurde die Festnahme
von 86 Juden gemeldet. Da das zur Verfügung stehende
G.fängnis Montluc überfüllt war, wurden die Juden in zwei
Räumen des Fort's Lamothe untergebracht. Bei Abtransport
der Juden an dem Bahnhof wurde festgestellt, dass nur
noch 84 vorhanden waren. Die Feststellungen ergaben, dass
zwei Juden am 11.2.43 in den frühen Vormittagsstunden, als
sie zum Austreten geführt wurden, entwichen sind. Die Auf-
sicht im Fort Lamothe wird von der Wehrmacht durchgeführt.

Bei den entwichenen Juden handelt es sich um
1.) L u x e n b u r g Aron, geb. 19.1.1893 in Lodz und
2.) D r i l l e r Siegfried, geb. 16.9.1896 in Wien.
Die angestellten Ermittlungen konnten bisher noch nicht
wieder zur Festnahme der beiden Juden führen.

Bei den nach dort gegebenen Briefumschlägen mit
Effekten und Wertgegenständen befinden sich auch die der
flüchtigen Personen.

Von Vorstehendem bitte ich Kenntnis zu nehmen.

Der Leiter des Einsatzkommandos:
i.V.

#-Obersturmführer.

Several reports and telexes signed by Barbie were found in the archives of the Office for Jewish Affairs of the Gestapo in Paris, the addressee. The three documents shown here concern a raid on the headquarters of the UGIF in Lyon, in which eighty-six Jews were arrested. Only one, the telex of February 11, 1943 (above left), is marked "Petr.," an abbreviation indicating that a subordinate had composed it. The other two documents show no such initials—Barbie himself both composed and signed them.

For complete English translations of these documents, see pages 132–33.

ENTREES (Melun)

MILER Jacques   F.O.   26.10.02 Paris   II, R.Tiquetone

ENTREES (LYON)

ANDERMANN Bronia	POL.	13.9.06 Buczacz	61, rue Voltaire
BACH Israel	POL.	9.6.89 Przemysl	80, R.Mercière
BLEUBERG Leizer	POL.	9.5.99 Borkohoff	7, r.Beaudelaire
BRUHL Wolf	POL.	1.12.80 Yaroslaw	II, rue de la Monnaie
CZERWONOGORA Chouma	POL.	21.5.11 Belchatow	R. du Boeuf
DICKMAN Sigmund	Pol.	21.9.09 Stanislau	54, C.La Fayette
DORNHEIM Gisèle	AP.	18.9.98 Vienne	RUFFIEUX (Savoie)
EIDEMANN Emmanuel	POL.	3.2.08 Pologne	208, R. Créqui
ENGEL Albert	ALL.	14.4.89 Berlin	17, R.Burdeau
ESSKREIS Jacob	Ex.Aut.	15.12.77 Lemberg	10, R. Fontes
EPELBAUM Israel	Pal.	1896 Nadimine	CUSSET (Isère)
ETLINGER Jacob	Ap.	20.8.03 Budapest	1, R.St.Poy- CALT...
FRYDMAN Icek	Pol.	25.6.01 Lodz	10, R. Persoz
FREUND Erna	Ex.All.	27.7.88 Erfurt	4, rue Jules Verne
FUHRER Osias	Ex.Aut.	22.2.90 Przelysl	5, R.Paul Bert
FUHRER Walter	Ex Aut.	22.11.04 Vienne	d°
FUCHS Georges	Hng.	25.8.05 Hidaskurt	ST.JULES les MARTEL
GORODISTEAN Michel	R.R.	10.2.01 Kichineff	115, rue Pierre Corne
GELBER Kalman	ROU.	1.3.00 Broholza	63, rue Rabelais
GRAD Henri	AUT.	15.5.99 Radlowicz	5, R.Paul Bert
GOTTLIEB Aurélie (POLTURAK)	POL.	11.6.95 Leow	145, R. Vendome
HIRSCHLER Frantz	Apa.	16.2.91 Mannheim	LE BOIS D'OINGT
HOROWICZ Isaac	Apa.	16.1.10 Przedborg	15, rue de la Frater...
KRUMAN Salomon	POL.	30.1.09 Bruxelles	20, rue Verte BRUXL.
LANDAU Ruchla	Ex Pol.	11.10.01 Chrzanow	5, rue Paul Bert
LANZET Anna (HERDORBER)	Apa.	10.8.00 Soloshov	5, rue de Fraternité
LANZET Malvine	Apa.	11.8.06 Vienne	d°
LEDERER Annie	Tch.	10.4.15 Jablontz	05, R. des Quatrefout... VILLEURB...
LICHTENSTEIN Sidonie (WEISBART)	Hng.	25.6.05 Ung.Brod.	14,Cours Lafayet...
LICHTENSTEIN Hans	Hng.	11.4.01 Ungsgerdohely	14 Cours Lafayette
LORBEL Efraim	Rou.	10.3.85 Armena	60, rue Rabelais
MAX Michael	Aut.	12.3.91 Allgersdorf	R.Garibaldi
MUNZER Norbert	Ex Aut.	30.8.08 Vienne	R. Garibaldi
MERKER Gerson	Aut.	29.8.88 Tyamienica	II, R.Burdeaux
RAPPAPORT Lola	Pol.	30.12.02 Czestochowa	17,R.Sully RO'N.E
RECKENDORFER Clara	ALL.	25.3.98 Nuremberg	7, r;Beaudelaire
RING Peiwel	Pol.	12.5.10 Nowy Sacz	ANICHE
ROKOTNITZ Marcus	Aut.	25.6.00 Manchtl	R. des Forges
REZNIK Alexandre	Let.	1.7.99 Riga	VILLEMAN
REIS Kurt	All.	3.2.01 Naremberg	5,R.D'Annonay
ROSENBACH Herta	Tch.	13.3.08 Hettstead	2, Montée du Gourgui...

The Klarsfelds were able to find among the archives from Drancy, in the possession of the YIVO Institute for Jewish Research in New York, this list of the eighty-six Jews arrested in the February 9, 1943, raid on the UGIF office in Lyon. Their names had previously been unknown. The same list, drawn up by the Gestapo in Lyon, was later found in the Archives de France. Two of the eighty-six Jews arrested escaped during the transfer to Drancy. The

Name		Nat.	Date	Place	Address
SAFRAN Menachem		TCH	29.8.00	Krosno	8, r. des 4 Colonnes
SCHNEEBAL Bernard		TCH	31.3.99	Kinty	63, r. des 4 Routes VILLEURBANNE
SZULKLAPER Rachmin		POL	2.9.11	Sosnovice	58 r. de la Gare de Lyon VILLEURBANNE
SZTARK Joseph		POL	6.6.11	Wolanow	Route de St-Cyr LYON
STEINMULLER Jules		POL	12.3.95	Lubartow	88, Bd. Magenta PARIS
SCHKIRA Simba		ROU	15.1.93	Roumanie	PERIGUEUX
SOUDAKOFF Joseph		R.R	25.7.90	Tchernigoff	113, r. Caulaincourt
STEIGMANN Betty		POL	9.9.06	Stridy	23 Gde Rue de la Guillotière
TLAGARZ Victor		POL	10.5.99	Lodz	72 r. Claude Decaen PARIS
TAUBMAN Feiwel	/	AUT	12.10.82	Snyalin	12 r. de l'Epée
TAUBMAN Beno		AUT	13.4.10	Cernovice	12 r. de l'Epée
TAUBMAN Salie (WISENTHAL)		AUT	18.9.79	Mielniza	12 r. de l'Epée
WOLF Elias		AUT	14.6.78	Starasol	5 r. des Petites Maries MARSEILLE
WEINSTOCK Herman		IND	2.1.96	Treza	5 r. Véricelle
JELEM Ryfka (SLOCHOWSKA)		POL	3.9.01	Smiatisch	12 r. Vieille Monnaie
PESKIND Jacques		F.N	7.8.81	Vilna	-
PERETZ Chaim		F.N	22.2.86	Sosnovice	-
ROSENSWEIG Chamja		F.N	3.6.17	Presbourg	-
AKIERMAN Berthe		F.N	20.10.21	Paris	5, Quai des Serins
BOLLACK Isidore		F.O	17.10.70	Sierentz	47 Cours de la Liberté
BRENDER Jules		F.N	26.7.98	Sastawna	60 r. St-Jean
BADINTER Simon		F.N	20.9.95	Pelenesti	7, R Quai Ml. Joffre
BLOCH Emmanuel		F.O	16.9.74	Niederodern	62 r. Hippolyte Karr
DOMNICZ Noel		F.N.--	3.10.20	Varsovie	BUZANCAIS (Indre)
DEUTCH André		F.N	14.3.09	Lugos	80 r. Frarieux
FELDHANDLER Salomon		F.N	28.8.08	Vienne	5 r. Dupuis PARIS
FREIDENBERG Pierre		F.O	11.7.01	Beaune	84 Av. Ml. Pétain
GRINBERG Esther		F.Op	16.10.10	Paris	51, r. Voltaire
GOLDBERG Joseph		F.N	15.11.07	Biola	5, Quai de Sorin
GUERIN Paul		F.O	1.12.29	Marseille	TALUIRS (près LYON)
GATTEGNO Régine		F.O	15.8.23	Lyon	133 r. Cuvier
JACOB Gilberte (LEVY)		F.O	25.1.13	Paris	40 R. Michel Servet
KOHN Samuel		F.O	12.7.01	Paris	14, Pl. Gabriel Rambaud
LANZENBERG Pierre		FR	3.7.00	Colmar	35 r. de Gd Taillis BRON
LOEB Marcelle		F.O	28.4.23	Strasbourg	12 Bd. Jules Favre
REIN Jean		F.O	28.2.20	Mulhouse	109, Av. Ernest Rulien LIMOGES
ROSEMBERG Abraham		F.N	12.11.88	Edinets	11 Av. Félix Faure
ROSENFELD Zeli		F.N	11.8.94	Kotselac	LA SOUTERRAINE (Creuse)
ROSENTHAL Irma (BAUMANN)		F.R	9.7.78	Illkirch	3 Pl. Aristide Briand
STEINBERG Armand		F.O	25.7.10	Paris	80 R. Mercière
SCHICK Madeleine		F.O	22.11.30	Colmar	18 Chemin Barthélémy
WEISSMANN Maier		F.N	5.12.85	Kaouzyna	25 Quai Claude Bernard.

-4-   12 Février 1943

ENTREES LYON (Suite)

WEILL Juliette	F.O	23.3.21 Strasbourg	6 Cours Lafayette

others were deported; only two of them survived. Among those deported was Simon Badinter, father of Robert Badinter, justice minister under French President François Mitterrand.

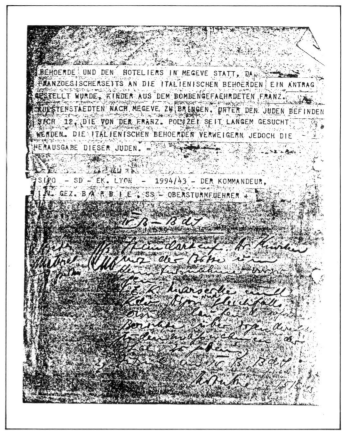

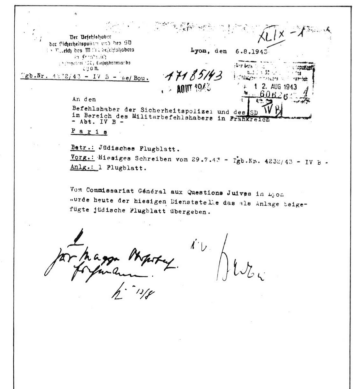

Three documents signed by Barbie concerning Jewish affairs. On the first line of the telex of May 15, 1943 (top), is the abbreviation "WE," which stands for either Welti or Wentzel, subordinates of Barbie who ordinarily dealt with Jewish affairs. (Welti was killed at the end of the summer of 1943 during a battle with partisans; Wentzel was killed in a bombing of the Gestapo offices in Lyon on May 26, 1944.) The letters WE are also on the memo of August 6, 1943 (above left); "Ba." for Bartelmus, another member of Department IV who was active in anti-Jewish operations, can be found on the memo of December 28, 1943 (above right). English translations of these documents can be found on page 133.

Paris le 24 Septembre 1971

DECLARATION

J'ai exercé à Lyon, à partir de Février 1943 jusqu'à la Libération en Août 1944, d'abord les fonctions de Directeur Régional de l'U.G.I.F. puis celle de Directeur Général pour la Zone Sud.

En Février 1943 la Section du Sicherheitsdienst commandée par BARBIE avait procédé à la " fermeture"des bureaux de l'U.G.I.F. alors installés Rue Sainte Catherine en arrêtant et en faisant déporter toutes les personnes qui étaient tombées sous la main des policiers allemands.

C'est à la suite de cette mesure que de nouveaux bureaux ont été ouverts à Lyon rue de l'Hôtel de Ville et que je fus dépêché depuis Marseille pour les diriger.

La Direction Régionale de l'U.G.I.F. à Lyon devenue après la dramatique fermeture des bureaux de Marseille, la Direction Générale pour la Zone Sud a accompli son véritable travail social en profondeur en liaison avec la Résistance Juive.

Nos bureaux officiels avec le personnel officiellement déclaré devaient rester en contact avec le Sicherheitsdiens? respectivement avec la Section commandée par BARBIE.

Certains de mes collaborateurs et moi-même étions ainsi appelés à la Gestapo ou nous nous y rendions de nous-mêmes lorsque nous tentions d'arracher aux griffes du Sicherheitsdienst telle ou telles personnes ou familles arrêtées.

Nous avons eu à faire ainsi soit à BARBIE lui-même soit plus volontiers à ses subordonnés lesquels ont été successivement pour les questions juives: un certain WELTI qui fut tué par le maquis, puis BARTHELMUS et BRUCKNER.

Si je me reporte de trente ans en arrière au climat dramatique de l'époque, je dois dire que nous avions tous l'intime conviction que ces tortionnaires dont dépendait la vie ou la mort de nos coréligionnaires, connaissaient parfaitement le sort redoutable qui attendait ceux qu'ils arrêtaient.

Je me souviens avoir vu BARBIE " écumer " en exhalant sa haine contre les juifs et l'expression " déporté ou fusillé c'est la même chose " est bien de lui. Elle est une de celle qu'il a prononcée devant moi et dont j'ai dû me faire l'écho auprès de mes collègues parisiens.   .../...

- 2 -

Dans cette ville de Lyon où mes collaborateurs et moi-même apprenions chaque jour quelque dramatique arrestation, suivie de déportation, l'heure de la Libération devait aussi être celle du châtiment.

Et l'on nous aurait vivement surpris, dans la situation d'extrême tension et d'extrême péril où nous vivions, qu'il pourrait en être autrement.

Raymond GEISSMANN

The late Raymond Geissmann. an attorney and, in 1943 and 1944, the director general of UGIF South, presented the Klarsfelds with the above affidavit in September 1971. His statement was submitted to the Munich prosecutor's office and played a key role in reopening the criminal investigation into Barbie's anti-Jewish activities.

DECLARATION

Between February 1943 and the liberation in August 1944, I held the position, in Lyon, first of regional director of the UGIF, then of director general for the South Zone.

In February 1943, the section of the SD commanded by Barbie effected the "closing" of the offices of the UGIF, then located on Rue Saint Catherine, by arresting and having deported all those who had fallen into the grip of the German police.

It was as a result of this measure that new offices were opened on Rue de l'Hôtel de Ville in Lyon, and that I was dispatched from Marseilles to direct them.

The regional office of the UGIF at Lyon, which became, after the tragic closure of the offices in Marseilles, the general headquarters for the South Zone, carried out its true mission of social welfare in cooperation with the Jewish Resistance.

Our official offices, with the staff that had been officially declared, were obliged to stay in contact with the SD and, in matters concerning it, with the section under the command of Barbie.

Certain of my colleagues and myself were thus summoned by the Gestapo or went there ourselves in the course of trying to wrest one person or another from the claws of the SD.

We thus had dealings either with Barbie himself, or, preferably, with his subordinates for Jewish matters, who were, in succession: Welti, who was killed by the partisans, then Barthelmus [sic] and Bruckner.

If I go back thirty years to place myself in the tragic climate of the time, I must say that we all had the deep-seated conviction that these torturers, on whom depended the lives and deaths of our coreligionists, knew perfectly well the terrible fate that awaited those whom they arrested.

I remember having seen Barbie "foam at the mouth" while giving vent to his hatred against the Jews, and the statement "deported or executed, it's the same thing" was certainly his own. It is something that he uttered in my presence, and that I must have repeated to my colleagues in Paris.

In this city of Lyon, where my colleagues and I learned each day of some tragic arrest, followed by deportation, the hour of liberation ought also to have been that of punishment.

And we would have been intensely surprised, in the situation of extreme tension and extreme peril in which we lived, that it could have turned out otherwise.

Raymond Geissmann

FRIEDEN MIT DEN VÖLKERN

STOPPT DIE BEGÜNSTIGUNG DER KRIEGSVERBRECHER

43 BÜRGER UND WIDERSTANDSKÄMPFER aus der französischen Stadt Lyon demonstrierten gestern vor dem Münchner Justizgebäude gegen die Einstellung des Verfahrens gegen den ehemaligen Gestapochef von Lyon, Klaus Barie. Eine Frau hält ein Bild ihrer nach Auschwitz deportierten Kinder in den Händen.
Funkbild: dpa

TWO MOTHERS OF IZIEU STRUGGLE TO BRING BARBIE TO JUSTICE

In Munich with Mrs. Benguigui—September 1971

On June 22, 1971, the office of the public prosecutor in Munich, which had been handling the Barbie case, decided to discontinue its investigation into the wartime activities of Klaus Barbie. Although Barbie's whereabouts was unknown, we saw his case as exemplary and felt we should speak out. "The French reaction would have to come from Lyon to have the greatest effect on German opinion," my wife, Beate Klarsfeld, recalls. "If no vigorous protests against this decision came from the place where Barbie had committed his crimes, the Germans would undoubtedly think the people of Lyon shared the Munich prosecutor's opinion. I had an idea in mind: the people of Lyon should stage a demonstration in Munich."

Beate, seeding French and German newspapers with interviews and data, produced a multitude of articles on both sides of the Rhine; together, we searched the archives of the CDJC in Paris, turning up new evidence against Barbie. The city of Lyon, the local branch of the LICA (Ligue Internationale Contre l'Anti-Sémitisme, or International League Against Anti-Semitism), members of Lyon's Jewish community, and several Resistance veterans promised to lend their support to the demonstration, which was scheduled for September 13. However, as the date drew near, the Lyon organizers began taking a deferential attitude toward West German authorities: they called upon the West German consul in Lyon, and were persuaded by him to limit the number of demonstrators to twelve. Such a demure protest, Beate feared, would make little impression on the West German public. She recalls:

The Germans were expecting flags, chests covered with decorations, a resolute entry by all the delegates into the court. They were expecting "the French Resistance"—that is, people stoutly demanding an end to the denial of justice to human rights. They were expecting fighters, not a few dozen Frenchmen no different from other tourists. This new development certainly seemed calculated to ruin the effectiveness of the trip.

Also, I knew that beside the documents I had collected, the delegation would take only a memorandum. Such a polite request for justice, it seemed to me, would not make much impression on a prosecutor; he would be swayed only by a forceful presentation of completely convincing documents. How could I make such a show of force all by myself?

Once more, the CDJC archives were of invaluable help. Among the children Barbie had arrested in the Jewish home at Izieu were three brothers: Jacques (thirteen years old), Richard (six years old), and Jean-Claude Benguigui (five years old). They had immediately been shipped to Drancy, as Barbie had stated in a telex to IV B in Paris, dated April 6, 1944.

I found the names of the Benguigui children on the list of the April 13, 1944, convoy destined for Auschwitz, where they were killed. The brother of other Izieu children whom Barbie had deported, Alexandre Halaunbrenner, was also named in the archives; we located him through the telephone directory. He knew Mrs. Benguigui, the mother of the three little boys, who lived in Paris at 33 rue des Francs-Bourgeois. I went to see her.

Mrs. Benguigui herself had been deported to Auschwitz on May 6, 1943, and was cruelly tortured in Block 10, where medical experiments were conducted. She had been declared seventy-five percent incapacitated, and her only source of income was a meager pension. While she was in the concentration camp, she kept hoping that her children were safe in the home at Izieu, but in the spring of 1944 she recognized her son Jacques's sweater in a pile of clothing that had belonged to recently gassed prisoners.

I told Mrs. Benguigui that the man responsible for the death of her children was being exculpated in Germany, and asked her if she felt up to going to Munich to make a protest that could turn out more successful than the delegation's. German public opinion could not fail to be stirred by this martyred mother. Since I foresaw that there would be no test of strength with the Munich court due to the slant of the delegation, we—Mrs. Benguigui and I—would have to deliver the necessary blow.

On September 12, the eve of the demonstration, I put Alexandre Halaunbrenner and Mrs. Benguigui on a train for Munich. In Lyon, Beate was being warned by a former Resistance fighter against accompanying the official delegation to the court; the French foreign minister, he said, was worried that any but a diplomatic approach might "disturb Franco-German relations." In Munich the next day, one of the delegation urged her not to enter the French consulate, pointing out that the public slap she had administered to West German Chancellor Kurt-Georg Kiesinger in protest of his Nazi past had made her a focus of controversy.

Right: Mrs. Fortunée Benguigui (right) demonstrating with Mrs. Beate Klarsfeld in Munich, 1971. The sign above their heads reads: "Prosecutor Rabl is whitewashing war criminals." Mrs. Benguigui holds in one hand a sign reading, "I will continue my hunger strike until the Munich prosecutor's office reopens proceedings against Klaus Barbie, the murderer of my three children," and in the other hand the photograph of her three sons reproduced alongside their biographical entry in this volume.

Page 112: German newspaper photograph of Beate Klarsfeld and Mrs. Benguigui demonstrating on the steps of the Palace of Justice in Munich. The caption reads: "43 citizens and Resistance fighters from the French city of Lyon demonstrated yesterday before the Palace of Justice against the dismissal of proceedings against the former head of the Gestapo in Lyon, Klaus Barie [sic]. A woman holds a photo of her children, deported to Auschwitz." The sign above Mrs. Benguigui's head says: "Stop aiding and abetting war criminals."

But Beate entered the consulate, stating: "I carry a French passport, I don't take orders, and I have as much right as you to enter a French consulate." Then, when the forty-eight visitors from France had finished a somewhat lengthy breakfast, she issued her call to arms:

The names of the twelve "official" delegates were read out, and they got up to go to the court. I did not restrain my indignation, for I knew the German reporters would be expecting fifty people.
"It would be a shame for us to stay here," I said. "We must all go together."
At the courthouse on Maxburgstrasse, the twelve "wise men" went into the building while the young people and I managed to lure the others out of the bus and at least mass them in front of the door. The reporters who encircled us were disappointed at the behavior of the French, who retreated in an orderly fashion when the doorman kept them from going into the court.
Everything had been worked out beforehand with the consulate and the German authorities. The demonstration made about one-tenth the stir it could have caused.
Upstairs in the chambers of Public Prosecutor Manfred Ludolph, who headed the department for Nazi crimes in Munich, the delegates submitted a "for your immediate attention" memorandum, which "solemnly requested" that the investigation be reopened. Ludolph listened politely, for he was under no real pressure, and he had been given no document capable of causing the original decision to be reexamined. So he promised nothing.
Meanwhile, Mrs. Benguigui and I had got inside the building, but since I could not get in to see Ludolph, I left him the file of documents Barbie had signed that we had found at the CDJC.

Included among these papers was a crucial affidavit we had received only days before. Beate continues:

In anticipation of the delegation's arrival in Munich, the spokesman for the prosecutor's office had let it be known that if new evidence was forthcoming, the case would be reopened. Proof was essential. The prosecutor's office would not be satisfied with motions, statements, or stands. It would not be enough for us to go to Munich; there would have to be at least sufficient evidence to allow the prosecutor's office to renew its investigation. Serge and I had settled down to this tedious

task, and examined innumerable documents at the CDJC in search of the trail of people who might have known Barbie.
Among many that had led nowhere because of a person's death or disappearance, an important one had turned up. I had noticed that the UGIF—that obligatory association that Kurt Lischka had created to represent the Jewish population before the French and the Occupation authorities—had a liaison office with the Gestapo's Office for Jewish Affairs (IV B). In 1943 and 1944 it was directed by a Jewish former lawyer from Berlin, Kurt Schendel, who had emigrated to France because of racial persecutions.
Schendel's task was often tragic, for he was in direct contact with the two architects of the Final Solution in France: Heinz Röthke, head of IV B, and Alois Brunner, one of Eichmann's deputies. I had thought that through his contacts with such SS leaders, Dr. Schendel might have been able to learn something about Barbie and what knowledge the regional Gestapo chiefs had of the fate of Jews shipped to Auschwitz.
Luck had been with us. There was a "K. Schendel" in the Paris telephone directory. I called his number daily, but no one answered until the evening of September 6. It was indeed the right Schendel.

We met with Schendel, who remembered Barbie although he had never seen him. On September 8, he gave us a deposition in German, in which he testified:

Even if the word "deportation" was avoided in official usage in favor of "fit for work," "evacuation," or "family reunification," in the course of the frequent meetings I was obliged to have with Röthke and Brunner I soon realized that "deportation" had dreadful connotations. Röthke and Brunner were frequently absent; I was told that they were "making reports in Berlin." When they returned to Paris, there were many conferences attended by representatives of IV B, of the commander of Paris, and of the commanders of other regions, with whom Röthke kept in constant touch by telephone.
Over the course of a year my observations of Department IV B and the numerous talks I had with those people as well as hints coming from other German bureaus completely convinced me that all of them, except perhaps the ones at the very bottom—but at least Röthke, Brunner, and the heads of the offices for Jewish Affairs of the regional Sipo-SD details—knew perfectly well what fate awaited the deportees.
I did not know Klaus Barbie personally, but I know that Barbie ordered the arrest of Jews in Lyon and took part in these arrests himself. I have seen reports stating that Barbie persecuted the Jews

with uncommon zeal. The UGIF branch in Lyon worked independently in the South Zone, and we were constantly in touch with it. Late in 1943 or early in 1944 we had a meeting in Paris with its directors, which I attended. There was a great deal of discussion of the summary executions at Fort Montluc of Jews whom Barbie had arrested. One of the delegates reported that ceaseless attempts had been made at least to keep arrested Jews from being shot, but that Barbie had replied: "Shot or deported, there's no difference."

That remark sticks in memory because at the time none of us could comprehend what he meant, and our anguish over the fate of the deportees became all the greater. So far as I am concerned, it was beyond doubt that the head of IV B in Lyon, which had the second largest Jewish population among French cities, was every bit as aware of the fate of the deportees as Röthke and Brunner. I might also add that Brunner assigned to several months' duty in Lyon his assistant, SS Oberscharführer Weiszel, who had been a member of Brunner's special commando force in Hungary and at Salonika, and who could give Barbie an eyewitness account of what happened to Jews deported to the East.

After leaving the documents for Ludolph, Beate helped the Association of German Victims of Nazism set up a press conference, while the French delegation went to visit the site of the former concentration camp at Dachau. As Beate recalls:

There was not enough time before the 5:30 P.M. plane to do both. Those who wanted to go to Dachau come what may had argued with those, including me, who wanted action to take priority. After all, the purpose of the delegation had to be explained to the German public. One of the Resistance veterans had almost come to blows with one of the young people. "What do you mean accusing me of just being a tourist?" he had demanded. "I was fighting in the Resistance before you were even born!" It was the same old argument, and it showed that the speaker did not believe in the future of the Resistance spirit.

In the end, there was a press conference, and the delegation went back to Lyon, where they were met at the airport as if they were the returning Argonauts by the mayor, the local elected officials, a television crew, and many townspeople.

Mrs. Benguigui and I were the only ones who stayed behind, ready to act, for the situation demanded it. Two women—one Jew, one German. Our ammunition: the only picture of her three children Mrs. Benguigui had, which I had had enlarged, and two signs I had made in our hotel room. Our plan was simple: on the following day we would stand on the street before the courthouse steps, where Mrs. Benguigui would hold up her children's picture and declare that she was beginning a hunger strike. The people of Munich would doubtless respond, and so would the papers and television. Mrs. Benguigui and I were going to stage a trial of strength with the prosecutor, however laughable our means of doing so.

We were there at nine o'clock the next morning. It was cold and rainy. We stood on crates I had got from a grocery store, and I had bought Mrs. Benguigui some heavy stockings and warm slippers.

By 5:00 P.M. there was a big crowd. Reporters and photographers turned out en masse. On the next day the German papers ran our pictures and long stories favorable to our effort. Young Germans were shouting: "It's a disgrace to our country for that poor woman to go to such lengths for justice." Women stroked Mrs. Benguigui's hair, and people went to buy her blankets. *France-Soir* dispatched a correspondent, who notified the French Consulate, and the vice-consul came with

a blanket. The police did nothing except warn us that the one of our signs might be actionable, but it stayed in plain sight.

At 6:00 P.M. Prosecutor Ludolph was still in his chambers, doubtless thinking: "How can I go home and leave that mother—who has been tortured directly, and through her children—behind on the steps? What if she is still there tomorrow? What if she gets sick during the night? If the sensation-hungry television news shows her still there at 3:00 A.M., there will be hell to pay over who left her to endure such inhuman conditions. A scapegoat will have to be found, and it may turn out to be me. Should I have her arrested? After what she has suffered already, that won't go down too well anywhere." Having analyzed the problem, the prosecutor decided to negotiate. The police politely escorted us to Ludolph's office.

Ludolph was about forty years old, impeccably dressed, and extremely cordial. "What do you want?" he asked.

"To have the investigation of Barbie reopened."

"I have to have conclusive proofs to do that," he said.

"Did you read the data I sent you yesterday?"

"I have not yet had time."

"Well, now is the time to do it."

When the prosecutor reached Schendel's affidavit, he exclaimed: "This is the sort of thing I was talking about. If Dr. Schendel's informant—the man who actually heard what Barbie said—can be produced, and if he confirms what Barbie is reported to have said, I promise I will reopen the case."

"Put that in writing for us."

"My secretary has gone for the day."

"That doesn't matter. I was once a typist myself."

I sat down at a typewriter, and Ludolph dictated an official letter in which he confirmed his promise. I gave it to the German reporters who were waiting below:

Dear Mrs. Benguigui:

As a result of our talk today I assure you that the material sent me on September 13 by the French delegation, Mrs. Klarsfeld, and yourself will be carefully studied. As to Dr. Schendel's affidavit of September 8, it seems to me necessary to locate the witness who told Dr. Schendel that the suspect said: "Shot or deported, there's no difference." If he can be found and will swear to that statement, I will be ready to reopen the investigation, for that will be proof that the suspect must at least have expected that his Jewish victims would be put to death.

Thank you for your visit. I send you my regards.

I almost dare to say that Mrs. Benguigui was happy. For the first time since the death of her children, she felt that she had done something for them. She had shown that she could act—better than so many others, who are glib of tongue, but less resolute when it comes to doing battle with law and custom.

Our luck held. Serge found the witness in the telephone directory. His name was Raymond Geissmann, and he was listed as a lawyer in the Court of Appeals, avenue Victor-Hugo in Paris. He proved indeed to be the same Raymond Geissmann who had been a director of the Lyon UGIF in 1943–44. When we met him, he told us that he had not been following the Barbie case because he had been on vacation until only a few days before.

But did he remember Barbie?

He certainly did. It was to him, and him alone, that Barbie made that dreadful remark. Geissmann immediately dictated to his secretary the affidavit that would cause the prosecution to be reopened [see document on page 111].

I then telephoned Ludolph to tell him that Jean Pierre-Bloch, president of LICA, and I were coming to Munich to hand him the affidavit. We made an appointment for October 1. To get publicity for this next step, the National Committee for the Pursuit and Punishment of War Criminals called a press conference for September 28. Pierre-Bloch was then authorized to carry out this action in the name of the fifty associations that comprised the committee. I notified the German papers, and Geissmann's testimony was printed in Munich. Pierre-Bloch's personality and position impressed the reporters, who were wondering whether the prosecutor would really reopen the case.

When we got off the plane, the press greeted us warmly, and so did representatives of the Victims of Nazism and the local chapter of B'nai B'rith. They went with us to Ludolph, who, along with his assistant, received us kindly. Ludolph read Geissmann's affidavit, which I had translated into German, and immediately dictated his decision to his secretary and gave us a carbon copy of it:

Munich, October 1, 1971

File No. 123 Js 5/71
(7 Js 61/65 Sta Augsburg)
Subject: Public prosecutor's penal investigation in the Augsburg Landgericht of Klaus Barbie for alleged complicity in murder.
1. The investigation will be reopened as to the charge against the defendant that he took part in the murders of French citizens of Jewish birth by deporting them from France to the East.
2. A decision on reopening the investigation in its entirety shall be postponed, but shall remain formally under advisement.

As to Barbie's repression of the Resistance, Ludolph commented that the Resistance veterans from Lyon had not yet sent him so many as one of the depositions they had promised to furnish. Nor did he conceal from us his personal opinion in the matter: "The page ought to be turned."

Speaking for the French Resistance, Pierre-Bloch replied that he could never accept such an attitude, and that the page would only be turned when Barbie had been tried for all the crimes he had committed in France.

Still, I could observe that a profound change had come over Ludolph within a few weeks. He had acknowledged the defeat of the Munich court's attempt to ensure legally that Barbie—and, through him, the other criminals whose cases his typified—go unpunished. He had been forced to reopen the investigation. I tried to figure out what he was up to, and what his line of thinking would be from then on.

Ludolph gave us two photographs, front and profile, that had been taken of Barbie in the early years of the war [see page 14], and another of a group of businessmen seated around a table, one of whom looked enough like Barbie as he might be twenty-five years later for the prosecution at Munich to assume it was he.

"The picture of this group," the prosecutor told us, "was taken in La Paz, Bolivia, in 1968. That is all I can say for the moment. Since you have demonstrated how effective you are, why don't you help me identify this man?"

Französische Jüdin beendete Hungerstreik

MÜNCHEN. Die 67jährige französische Jüdin Fortune Benguigni hat ihre Hungerdemonstration wegen der Einstellung des Verfahrens gegen den früheren Lyoner Gestapochef Klaus Barbie vor dem Gebäude der Münchner Staatsanwaltschaft nach eintägiger Dauer am Mittwoch beendet. Auch Beate Klarsfeld, die mitdemonstrierte, zog sich zurück.

Nach Mitteilung des bayerischen Justizministeriums vom Mittwoch verzichtete die Französin auf die Fortsetzung ihres Hungerstreiks, nachdem sie von dem Leiter der Abteilung für NS-Verbrechen bei der Münchner Staatsanwaltschaft, Dr. Manfred Ludolf, empfangen und über die Handlungsweise der Staatsanwaltschaft im Fall Barbie informiert worden war. Fortune Benguigni gab Oberstaatsanwalt Dr. Ludolf einen Zeugen an, der bestätigen soll, daß Barbie persönlich an Tötungen beteiligt war. Sie erklärte sich bereit, die Münchner Staatsanwaltschaft bei der Suche nach dem Zeugen zu unterstützen. Sollte dieser Zeuge entsprechend aussagen, dann könne dies Anlaß zu neuen Maßnahmen der Staatsanwaltschaft sein, sagte ein Justizsprecher. Unser Bild zeigt Fortune Benguigni während ihres Hungerstreiks.

French Jew Ends Hunger Strike

Munich. The 67-year-old French Jew Fortune Benguigni [sic] Wednesday ended the hunger strike she had begun one day before in front of the building housing the Munich prosecutor's office in protest against the cessation of proceedings against the former head of the Lyon Gestapo, Klaus Barbie. Beate Klarsfeld, who was with her, also ended her demonstration.

According to a communiqué from the Bavarian justice ministry Wednesday, the Frenchwoman called a halt to her hunger strike after she had been received by Dr. Manfred Ludolph, the head of the department for Nazi crimes of the Munich public prosecutor's office, and had been briefed on the way the prosecutor's office had been handling the Barbie case. Fortune Benguigni indicated a witness to Public Prosecutor Ludolph that could allegedly establish that Barbie personally took part in killings. She declared her readiness to support the Munich public prosecutor's office in the search for the witness. Should the witness testify accordingly, the testimony could occasion new measures on the part of the prosecutor's office, a Justice Ministry spokesman said. Our photo shows Fortune Benguigni during her hunger strike.

In La Paz with Mrs. Halaunbrenner—March 1972

Beate took Ludolph's photos to an expert in anthropometry. As a result of his verdict—that, "in all likelihood" the La Paz businessman and Klaus Barbie were one and the same—the Munich prosecutor was even more eager to work with us. In November, Ludolph supplied the name of a German living in Lima, Peru, who thought he could identify Barbie. In the closing days of 1971, we received not only a Peruvian address for Barbie, but his alias: Klaus Altmann.

Three weeks later, the Paris newspaper *L'Aurore*, using information and photos we provided, ran a story under the headline: "Former Nazi Klaus Barbie Has Just Taken Refuge in Peru After a Long Stay in Bolivia—Is France Going to Demand Him?" The cry for extradition rose in France; Altmann, responding from his newly purchased second home in Lima, vigorously denied that he was Barbie. Armed with written evidence she and Ludolph had assembled, Beate readied for a trip to Lima—only to learn, on the very day of her flight, that Barbie would soon drive across the border into Bolivia.

After placing detailed stories in the Peruvian press, Beate flew from Lima to La Paz and repeated the performance: the Bolivian papers of Sunday, January 30, 1972, were plastered with the headline "He's Not Altmann, He's Barbie." By Tuesday, word had come that the French were requesting extradition. Beate, harassed by Bolivian officials throughout her short stay, was told to leave the country the following morning; however, Immigration Minister Rudolfo Greminger, charged with reporting to the Bolivian Supreme Court on the Barbie case, asked her to return to Munich for more information on Barbie's background. "I need those new documents, and you are the only one who can get them for me," were Greminger's parting words. "I have decided to work with you, as I have just informed the press."

In early February, Barbie was arrested in Bolivia on a fraud charge, raising hopes that if information could be supplied quickly enough to the right people in Bolivia, he might be held in jail. Although Barbie was released on February 12, after a few days' detention, Beate planned a return to La Paz. In addition to supplying Greminger with documents, Beate recalls, she had a second aim in mind:

I had seen that so far as the Peruvians and the Bolivians were concerned, former Nazis were only political refugees like any others. Scarcely anyone in South America knew about the Gestapo's work of extermination. They had to be shown in a dramatic way that Barbie was not what he said he was: "a soldier who had only done his duty." Barbie had told a reporter: "During the war I acted like any other officer of an army in combat, just like the Bolivian army officers fighting Ché Guevara's guerillas." Emphasis, therefore, had to be put on the massacres of civilians and the liquidation of Jews. Mrs. Benguigui's example had, it seemed to me, been conclusive: the Bolivians would have to see something more than documents and photographs. They had to come into direct contact with the evil of Nazism by encountering someone whom Barbie himself had caused to suffer.

In the end, Beate approached Alexandre Halaunbrenner's mother, whom Barbie had struck with his pistol when he came to the family's home on October 24, 1943, to arrest her husband and older son—and who, according to Alexandre, had recognized Barbie immediately from a recent newspaper photograph and would thus be able to identify him. Again Beate recalls the circumstances:

Mrs. Halaunbrenner was soon to be sixty-eight years old. Her life had been sad and trying. As with Mrs. Benguigui, Barbie had turned her life into one long period of mourning. Her husband, her older son, and two of her daughters had been killed by Barbie. Only Alexandre and one daughter, Monique, were left.

In spite of her age, the altitude of La Paz, and the suspense of waiting to face Barbie, Mrs. Halaunbrenner was not afraid. She knew she was going to be useful and that from her mouth the Bolivians would learn how Barbie had persecuted innocent people. On Thursday evening, February 17, she told me she would go, and so I set our departure for Sunday.

I asked Ludolph for copies of pictures of Mrs. Barbie from 1940 that he had just uncovered, and I flew to Munich. Ludolph gave me the photographs, which were quite conclusive evidence: Frau Barbie had scarcely changed in thirty years, and had hardly any wrinkles. There was no doubt about the resemblance—it jumped right off the paper.

As soon as Serge saw the photographs at the airport in Orly, he dragged me into a taxi. It was almost midnight when we got to the offices of *L'Aurore*. The layout of the paper was changed, and the two photographs and a long story, "The Final Proof," inserted. On Saturday, I got thirty copies made of the two pictures and of the one of the Halaunbrenner family before the tragedy. I intended them for the Bolivian authorities and especially for the Bolivian newspapers so that they could complete their stories as soon as I got there.

We left Paris on Sunday evening, February 20. Nothing untoward happened on our flight to Lima, where I decided to remain for a day. I was afraid Bolivia might turn us away; that would be less likely to happen if the Peruvian papers had already run my latest proofs and Mrs. Halaunbrenner's story. We were met by a group of reporters, who almost snatched the pictures of Mrs. Barbie and the Halaunbrenner family away from me. Mrs. Halaunbrenner answered the deluge of questions simply and with dignity, though she was a little at sea. She had not expected such attention from the press nor thought that her story would ever create such excitement. Now she recognized how necessary her trip was.

The next day the Lima papers devoted a large part of their front page to our story and pictures. I also talked with a correspondent of an American newspaper who was on his way to La Paz to interview Colonel Banzer.

At eight o'clock on Tuesday morning we were at the the airport, where we were made to wait at the baggage check-in. Then we were told that a telegram had come from La Paz denying us permission to enter and instructing us to get in touch with the Bolivian Embassy. The Bolivian consul saw everything that happened at the airport. The American correspondent boarded the plane, saying he was sorry he would not be able to talk to us on the way. We picked up our luggage again and took a taxi straight to the Bolivian Embassy, where the ambassador told us we would have to apply for a visa to the Ministry of the Interior and the Foreign Ministry by means of a telegram with the reply prepaid.

When we got back to our hotel, I sent the two telegrams, plus one to Greminger to remind him that it was he who had asked me to return. There was nothing to do now but wait, and our hopes sank. Mrs. Halaunbrenner was truly in despair over having come so far, only to be kept from entering Bolivia.

We still had close contacts with the newspapers, which started a campaign on the theme: the Bolivians are protecting Barbie by denying his accusers the right to demand justice in Bolivia.

I went back alone to the Bolivian consulate as soon as it opened on Wednesday; still no answer. About 5:00 P.M. Agence France Presse (AFP) telephoned me that there had been a dramatic event in La Paz. The Bolivian minister of the interior had released a statement saying that Colonel Banzer himself had granted us a visa, that the Altmann papers were currently being studied in the foreign ministry (and also in the Ministry of the Interior), and that the legal authorities would reach a decision in due course.

I dashed to the Bolivian consulate with the AFP dispatch, but was told that nothing had come through yet. The consul, Ricardo Ríos, a great friend of Barbie, seemed overjoyed at giving me a negative answer. I was hardly back at the hotel, however, when he called me to say that he had just got our authorization. This time it was I who was overjoyed: "Now you see I was right to keep on hoping."

We arrived in La Paz on Thursday at 12:30 P.M. I was worried about how Mrs. Halaunbrenner would stand the altitude, but she seemed to take it better than I. As soon as the plane landed, a young man came aboard to tell me that I had to promise not to make any statements to the newspapers or I would be expelled at once.

I played along with him, since I could not do otherwise, but I had no intention of keeping a promise that had been extorted from me. I would have betrayed my cause if I had kept my word.

Albert Brun, the AFP correspondent in Lima, had been in La Paz since Barbie was released from jail. He met us and took us to the Hotel La Paz, where I promised the disappointed reporters that I would see them soon.

I tried to see Greminger, but it appeared that he had had his wrist slapped. "I no longer have anything to do with the Barbie case," he said. "You will have have to see Deputy Foreign Minister Jaime Tapia." Tapia gave me an appointment for 3:30 P.M. on Friday.

Things now seemed all in Barbie's favor. The presidential spokesman, Alfredo Arce, stated: "There are to be no proceedings for extraditing Klaus Altmann. President Banzer thinks he has enough legal evidence to consider the problem settled."

A few days earlier, Constancio Carrion, Bolivia's leading expert on international law as it applies to private citizens, and also a counselor of the Foreign Ministry, had stated: "Bolivia is an inviolable asylum, and all who take refuge in it are sacrosanct. The time limit for the prosecution of major crimes in Bolivia is eight years. Altmann-Barbie's are, therefore, ancient history. The petty deception that Barbie practiced by disguising himself as Altmann is at the most punishable in Bolivia by a small fine."

Carrion was also one of the lawyers who were handling Barbie's defense.

On Friday morning the American correspondent invited us to breakfast at the city's best restaurant. He told me: "While I was talking with Colonel Banzer on Wednesday, I told him what a bad impression he would make on international opinion by preventing these two brave women from entering Bolivia. Banzer reacted favorably to that, for he is sensitive to American opinion. The CIA, it appears, pays him seven dollars a day for every prisoner he keeps in confinement for political reasons. That money allows him to pay his army, which is always disgruntled."

In the afternoon, we went to Jaime Tapia's office, and I gave him my new proofs. Mrs. Halaunbrenner wept as she told him about her family. He patted her kindly on the shoulder and promised that he would try everything, but we knew what that meant. At any rate, we had kept within the law and furnished the proper authorities with data, and so far had not met with the press.

On Saturday, February 26, I tactfully sounded out the reporters. They had instructions not to say anything about our presence. Only a more concrete development would give them a chance to publicize what we had to say and show. My idea of a press conference delighted them, especially as I proposed showing a film of Barbie's victims reacting to an interview that had been made with Barbie when he was in jail and shown on French television. So I had to dash around madly but discreetly to find an adequate projector.

On Sunday, while we were walking on the Prado, Mrs. Halaunbrenner suddenly heard two women chatting in Yiddish, and she lost no time introducing herself. Her new friends were already aware of why we were there, and invited us to luncheon and to spend the afternoon at their home.

A dispatch alarmed my family and friends in France: "Two men not identified as policemen are reported to have taken B.K. away." This rumor must have reached the Bolivian government, for during the afternoon the Reuters correspondent was let into the office where I was being confined to determine that I had not been kidnapped.

I spent the day in that office with the same food as before, which I did not touch, trying in vain to find out why I was being kept there. A detective who spoke a little French got so annoyed at my constant questions that he replied in the rather basic and vigorous words he had learned of the language of Descartes: "You've given us a royal pain in the ass, so we're going to do the same for you until you just buzz off!"

After that I resigned myself to my fate, and I waited patiently until evening, when the office closed and I was released as on the previous day.

Meanwhile, at my instigation, French Ambassador Jean-Louis Mandereau made a formal request for a confrontation between Barbie and Mrs. Halaunbrenner. Barbie, of course, stubbornly refused, and Tapia told Mandereau on Wednesday morning that it would be impossible to force him to consent. Barbie's refusal was significant. As for

Beate Klarsfeld (left) and Ita-Rosa Halaunbrenner (right) at the airport in Paris before leaving for Bolivia in 1972. Also pictured are Mrs. Halaunbrenner's daughter Monique and son Alexandre.

meeting him myself, I did not see what good that would do, any more than meeting any of my other adversaries.

We then tried to initiate legal proceedings against Barbie, with Mrs. Halaunbrenner pressing charges as an individual for the murder of four of her family. The first lawyer we approached, Jaime Mendizabal, turned us down for political reasons: his brother was in the government. (Later his brother would resign, and he himself would be arrested.) The second, Manuel Morales Dávila, agreed, and began proceedings by registering Mrs. Halaunbrenner's complaint with a notary. Then he told us his fee: seven thousand dollars. Seeing that we were the object of a blockade, I told the press, "Bolivian justice is too expensive for us."

On Saturday we went with our Jewish friends to Lake Titicaca for a rest before undertaking our protest demonstration. That morning I bought chains and two padlocks.

On Monday morning, March 6, I got our passports in order, procured an exit visa from the Ministry of the Interior, and reserved seats on the 8:00 P.M. flight to Lima. About noon we fastened the chains around our waists and wrists, and, carrying two signs in Spanish, we headed for the offices of the Transmaritima Boliviana, of which Barbie was the managing director. We sat down on a bench directly opposite the offices, which were located on the Prado, the busiest street in La Paz. Then we chained ourselves to the bench and began waving our signs. A crowd gathered, and cars slowed down or stopped.

There was a traffic jam. There had not been a demonstration right in the middle of town for some time: since his putsch in August, Banzer had kept La Paz in his iron grip. The news was broadcast over the radio, and that drew even more people. A police jeep arrived; its occupants read our signs and went away.

At 4:00 P.M. a small truck drew up, and men in civilian dress jumped out and mingled with the bystanders. Suddenly they leaped on us, snatched our signs, and took to their heels. Some young Bolivians and an Israeli tourist quickly made us new signs.

A Bolivian woman wearing a poncho and carrying her baby on her back said: "There is no such thing as justice in Bolivia. Kidnap him or kill him."

A reporter held a microphone in front of me and asked what the chains signified.

"They are the chains that bind Bolivia to Nazism," I said.

It began to rain. Mrs. Halaunbrenner, whose courage was extraordinary, could take no more. I, too, was exhausted. We had been on our bench for six hours and seen a good part of the population of La Paz, including the diplomatic corps, file past us. One of the French Embassy staff stopped in front of us to say: "What you are doing won't accomplish anything."

Nevertheless, the reverberations of our protest and our appeal to the Bolivian people would be great and positive in the press and, I believed, also among the public, judging from the sympathy expressed by those who had come to watch us.

That evening we boarded our plane, and then spent twenty-four hours in Lima, which was pleasantly warm after La Paz. We had to get Mrs. Halaunbrenner back into shape, for she had caught a cold.

We went to a hairdresser, as we wanted to be looking our best before the television cameras that would be waiting for us at Orly, and then gave the Peruvian press a full account of all we had accomplished. Then we flew to Paris, where we landed on Thursday afternoon, March 9, eighteen days after we had started out.

119

A report in a Bolivian newspaper on the campaign waged against Barbie by Mrs. Halaunbrenner and Beate Klarsfeld in February 1972 in La Paz:

To Establish That Altmann Is Barbie
Nazi Huntress Brings Living Proof from Paris
Beate Klarsfeld, better known as the "Nazi Huntress," arrived yesterday in Lima, bringing with her "living proof" that Klaus Altmann is Klaus Barbie —Mrs. Ita Halaunbrenner—as well as a photograph of the wife of the Nazi war criminal that exhibits features coinciding with that of the German exterminator. Klarsfeld will travel today to La Paz.

The "living proof," as Mrs. Klarsfeld has described her companion, arrived with her "to identify Barbie definitively," revealed the tenacious nemesis of the murderers of the French Resistance in Lyon, France.

For her part, Mrs. Halaunbrenner said yesterday that "Klaus Altmann is in reality Klaus Barbie," and that she would unmask him in La Paz. Meanwhile, Altmann or "Barbie" is at this moment in the capital of Bolivia, under close surveillance stemming from his recent arrest, not due to suspicions as to his identity but for nonpayment of various taxes to the Bolivian government.

Ita Halaunbrenner, as she declared before leaving for Lima and La Paz, and as she confirmed yesterday, lost her husband and three children during the French Resistance in Lyon, and she herself suffered physically in October 1943 the tortures that Barbie personally administered—according to her statement—after she was arrested by the Nazi war criminal.

Mrs. Klarsfeld, in addition, revealed that she had brought other proof that Altmann is "Barbie," proof that she has secured since the last time she was in Lima and La Paz—three weeks ago—pursuing

the Germano-Bolivian who has now been turned into a pursued Nazi.

Beate Klarsfeld will continue her journey today to Bolivia, together with her companion. The Peruvian police have provided her with heavy security since her arrival on the nation's soil.

Klarsfeld yesterday urged Altmann publicly through the press to submit himself to French justice so that it may be clarified whether, as he says, he is not "Barbie."

She also said that he would have every guarantee of an opportunity to clear himself, and will receive the necessary protection during the trial.

This she said while reading a document in French, which begins by saying: "Now that the Klaus Altmann mask has been uncovered"—which was recently revealed in Lima, and will be disseminated through Agence France Presse. She also revealed that the children of Mrs. Halaunbrenner had barely reached fifteen years of age when they were killed, and that she hoped that this time the Bolivian government would proceed as the French people hope, even more so with the proof that she is now bringing on her second trip to La Paz.

Caption, photo left: The photograph of the wife of the war criminal Klaus Barbie maintains a similarity to the facial features of the wife of Altmann. The Nazi Huntress showed them yesterday upon her arrival in Lima. Today she will travel to La Paz to continue the proceedings.

Caption, photo right: Beate Klarsfeld, better known as the Nazi Huntress, accompanied by the living proof she brought from France, Mrs. Ita Halaunbrenner, during the press conference which the two held for the Lima press.

Opposite: An article from a La Paz newspaper dated February 29, 1972:

Klaus Barbie Wrote from Bolivia:
"Write to Me in the Name of Mayer or of Altmann"
Moving Plea of Itt Halaumbrenner [sic]
After the end of World War II, Klaus Barbie wrote from La Paz to his family living in Strassenbergen, Germany, telling them that from that date on they should write to him in the name of Altmann or Mayer, Beate Klarsfeld claimed at a press conference last evening.

In an open challenge to the immigration authorities, who had warned her not to make declarations to the media, the Nazi Huntress declared that there are irrefutable proofs that establish that Altmann and Barbie are the same person.

Nevertheless, when she was asked whether she had Barbie's fingerprints in her possession, she said they are not in the archives, since in Germany only those with previous arrest records have their fingerprints on file.

Klarsfeld said she was confident that Bolivian justice would proceed with the expulsion of Altmann, accused of being the chief of the Nazi Gestapo in Lyon during the German occupation.

Grilled by the gentlemen of the press, Beate Klarsfeld said that if she is expelled from Bolivia, it will demonstrate that Bolivia is covering for a war criminal. "I trust that President Banzer, who had a German grandfather, will try to reinstate the good name of Germany and will proceed with justice. I do not believe that Mrs. Halaumbrenner could have come this far and will not be permitted a confrontation with Altmann so she can verify his double identity," she said.

Finally, she noted that Altmann's claim about

Klaus Barbie escribió desde Bolivia:

"ESCRIBANME AL" NOMBRE DE MAYER O DE ALTMANN"

CONMOVEDOR PEDIDO DE ITT HALAUMBRENNER

Klaus Barbie, escribió a sus familiares radicados en Strassenbergen—Alemania desde La Paz, luego de terminada la segunda guerra mundial, recomendando que a partir de esa fecha dirigieran a nombre da Altmann o Mayer. Afirmó Beate Klarsfeld en rueda de prensa efectuada en la víspera.

En franco desafío a las autoridades de inmigración que le advirtieron no efectuar declaraciones a los medios de difusión, la "cazadora" de nazis, manifestó que existen pruebas irrefutables que comprueban que Altmann y Barbie son la misma persona.

Sin embargo al ser consultada sobre si tenía en su poder las huellas dactilares de Barbie, dijo que estas no existían en los archivos ya que en Alemania solo los prontuariados tienen fichas de huellas dactilares.

TESTIGO

En forma conmovedora e interrumpida por sollozos y lágrimas, Itt Rosa Halaumbrenner (foto derecha) relató la forma en que fue apresado su esposo y su hijo de 13 años por Klaus Barbie los cuales fueron posteriormente muerto y deportando por la gestapo de Lyon.

Itt Halaumbrenner, demandó justicia de parte de las autoridades bolivianas, manifestando que no sólo se arrestó a miembros de la resistencia sino que se ensañó con niños y mujeres por el solo hecho de ser judíos.

Concluida la conferencia de prensa, la Klarsfeld fue conducida a las oficinas de la INTERPOL, donde se le recordó las normas existentes para los turistas y le fue sugerida la posibilidad de que a través de la Embajada de

Sin embargo se refirió al caso Altmann señalando: "Sabemos en París que la respuesta del gobierno boliviano acerca de la extradición que hemos solicitado para Klaus Altmann, demandará algún tiempo. En realidad, Altmann está en poder de la justicia boliviana".

---

the date of his birth—October 15, 1915, in Berlin—has been proven false, because in the records of that city there is no one with that name registered on that date.

Witness

In a moving manner and interrupted by sobs and tears, Itt Rosa Halaumbrenner (photo right) recounted the way in which her husband and her thirteen-year-old son—one subsequently killed, and one deported, at the hands of the Lyon Gestapo—were arrested by Klaus Barbie.

Itt Halaumbrenner demanded justice from Bolivian authorities, showing that he not only arrested members of the Resistance, but raged against children and women for the sole reason that they were Jews.

At the conclusion of the press conference, Klarsfeld was conducted to the offices of Interpol, where she was reminded of the regulations in force for tourists, and where the possibility was suggested to her that a confrontation between Altmann and Mrs. Halaumbrenner be requested through the French Embassy.

Interior Ministry

The Ministry of the Interior will pronounce itself today regarding the situation of the Nazi Huntress Beate Klarsfeld, according to the Under Secretary for Immigration, Rodolfo Greminger.

It was announced before her entry into the country that in conformity with the regulations governing the matter, the status of tourist—which was the visa granted to Klarsfeld—prohibited her from making declarations while within the nation's borders. Greminger said that a final determination on the stance of the Huntress will be announced today.

Ambassador

French Ambassador Jean-Louis Mandereau, questioned on this same issue, said: "I have no opinion in this matter."

Nevertheless, he made reference to the Altmann case, noting: "We know in Paris that the reply of the Bolivian government on the extradition which we have requested for Klaus Altmann will take some time. In reality, Altmann is in the hands of Bolivian justice."

At Orly, a crowd of friends, reporters, and cameramen rushed up to welcome us home. We did not have Barbie in our bags, but for a while we had represented the insatiable quest for justice. Into the myth that a criminal, by fleeing to the ends of the earth, could escape retribution, two women—one belonging to a murderous people, the other to its martyrs—had intruded, going to the other side of the globe to find him and demand justice.

On Monday morning I summoned all the reporters by telephone to a press conference at 11:00 A.M. I had to act quickly; if I waited even until afternoon, the police might stop everything. At 10:15, half a dozen plainclothesmen entered the hotel. Two came up to me in the lobby and asked me to follow them to police headquarters. I went upstairs to get a few things from my room, and found two policemen standing guard outside it. I telephoned our Jewish friends to come and comfort Mrs. Halaunbrenner, who was terribly worried. I also alerted Bruno so that he could explain to the reporters what had happened if I did not return by eleven.

Major Tito Vargas, the head of the Bolivian security police, whom I already knew from my first visit to La Paz, solemnly warned me against holding a press conference and said that if I did, I would be thrown out of the country once and for all.

I went back in a police jeep at 10:50 A.M., and we held our press conference in a large room in the hotel. About thirty reporters attended. I showed the film and handed out photographs and press kits that Serge had prepared. Then Mrs. Halaunbrenner took over, and her story of her martyrdom as a woman and a Jewish mother deeply moved the reporters. When she finished speaking at 12:15, the policemen who had been there in the morning came back and took me off to police headquarters again. They shut me up in a filthy little office and gave me some very salty soup and a plate of something or other. I sat there rotting until 5:00 P.M. Then the chief of the Policia Internacional, Hernán Arteaga, let me go with instructions to keep my mouth shut thereafter. "This is the last warning," he said. "Otherwise you will be arrested."

On Tuesday there was only one topic in the papers—our conference. And they played it to their hearts' content: the blackout had been punctured. Whole pages were devoted not only to the conference, but also to the extermination camps, thus showing readers what the vacuous face of Altmann-Barbie had concealed from them.

When we went out, Bolivians came up to us and offered their sympathy to Mrs. Halaunbrenner, telling us that they were on our side and that Barbie ought to be extradited.

After breakfast on Tuesday, February 29, two familiar faces suddenly reappeared. I got up to do my turn at police headquarters, telling Mrs. Halaunbrenner to go to our Jewish friends.

On March 6, 1972, Beate Klarsfeld and Ita-Rosa Halaunbrenner chained themselves to a bench opposite Klaus Barbie's office building in the center of La Paz to demonstrate for Barbie's extradition. The sign held by Beate reads, "In the name of the millions of victims of Nazism, let Klaus Barbie-Altmann be extradited"; Mrs. Halaunbrenner's says, "People of Bolivia, help me! Mothers, I ask only for justice. May Barbie-Altmann, murderer of my husband and three of my children, be judged." (Gamma photos)

BRINGING BARBIE BACK

In November 1972, anticipating that Bolivia would turn down France's request for the extradition of Klaus Barbie, the French philosopher Régis Debray, my wife, and I devised a plan to return the former Lyon Gestapo chief by force. We would capture Barbie in Bolivia with the help of Bolivian officers, opponents of Hugo Banzer's dictatorship, and bring him out through the Chile of Salvador Allende. I met up with Debray in Santiago; in the last days of 1972, we chartered a small plane and joined our Bolivian contact, Gustavo Sanchez Salazar, at the Bolivio-Chilean border.

Our carefully prepared kidnap plan was never carried out. In March 1973, Barbie was taken into custody by Bolivian authorities, who feared he might flee before the country's Supreme Court could decide on his extradition. When Barbie was released upon the court's refusal to extradite in October 1973, it was too late—weeks earlier, Chile had fallen into the hands of Augusto Pinochet.

Nine years would pass before returning Barbie to face charges in Europe again seemed a possibility. The inauguration of a socialist president, Hernán Siles Zuazo, had put an end to the long line of rightist dictators in Bolivia. Nevertheless, the Bolivian Supreme Court, controlled by judges appointed during the era of dictatorship, would almost certainly reject any request for Barbie's extradition.

Another avenue presented itself: Barbie had a ten-year-old debt to the Bolivian state mining corporation—an account that he, in a characteristic display of bravado, refused to square in the manner prescribed. Barbie was imprisoned in La Paz in January 1983.

Once again, our good friends Régis Debray and Gustavo Sanchez Salazar proved invaluable. Sanchez was the newly appointed Under Secretary of the Interior in Bolivia, and Debray was now one of the two special advisors to French President François Mitterrand, who was himself faithful to the memory of Resistants and deportees, having been a member of the Resistance during the war.

Above: Meeting at the border of Chile and Bolivia in December 1972 are, left to right, Régis Debray, Gustavo Sanchez Salazar, a friend of Sanchez, and Serge Klarsfeld. In the background, the small chartered plane that had brought Debray and Klarsfeld from Santiago, Chile. Opposite: Finally, after ten years, Gustavo Sanchez Salazar oversees the transfer of Barbie to the airplane that will take him to French Guyana, the first stop on his forced return to France.

On the evening of February 4, 1983, Sanchez picked up Klaus Barbie at the La Paz prison where he was being held and brought him to a nearby airfield for a short flight to French Guyana, where a French jet was waiting. For Sanchez had obtained the cancellation of Barbie's Bolivian citizenship and the decision to expel him—and not in a direction which would be chosen by Barbie.

Barbie was flown immediately back to France and imprisoned in Lyon's Fort Montluc, the same jail to which he had sent the forty-four children of Izieu for internment before their deportation and death. He remains in Lyon today, awaiting, after forty-one years, final retribution for his crimes against humanity.

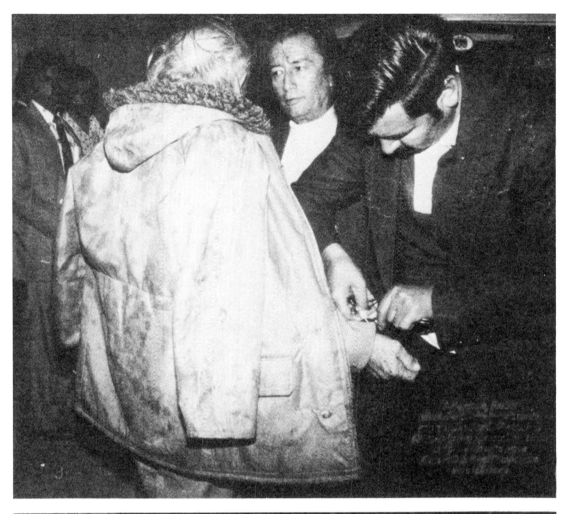

EJERCITO DE BOLIVIA
CEDULA MILITAR E IDENTIDAD PERSONAL
TCNL. AD-HONOREN
Grado, Arma o Servicio
KLAUS ALTMANN HANSEN
Nombre Completo
Nacido el 25 Oct 15   Grupo sangre "O"
D   M
Rh —
Firma del Portador
Válido hasta 31-XII-85   No.

33300252

Est. Civil Casado......
Color de la Piel Blanca......
Ojos Verdosos Est. 1.70
Señales Part. Ninguna......
....
PULGAR DER.
Jefe del Dpto. II EMGE.
Queda anulado el 31-XII-85

BARBIE'S TIES TO
THE SPECIAL SERVICES
OF THE BOLIVIAN
DICTATORSHIP

The original of this military identification card (opposite) which shows Barbie wearing the uniform of the Bolivian Special Services, is in our possession. The card was issued by the Bolivian Army in the name of Klaus Altmann Hansen, Barbie's initial false identity; it lists Barbie as two years younger than he is, and gives his rank as honorary lieutenant colonel. The fingerprint is definitely Barbie's own.

Valid through December 31, 1985, the I.D. was issued in 1980, under the terrible dictatorship of General Luis Garcia Meza. It is signed on the back by Colonel Luis Arce Gomez, minister of the interior and head of Department II, Intelligence. Both Garcia Meza and Arce Gomez are currently fugitives, wanted by both Bolivia and the United States due to their implication in the smuggling of Bolivian cocaine into the United States.

Left: Colonel Luis Arce Gomez (far right), minister of the interior in 1980 under the dictatorship of General Luis Garcia Meza (second from left). Opposite: Front and back of the Bolivian military identification card issued to Barbie under the name of Klaus Altmann Hansen.

THE CHILDREN REMEMBERED

Mrs. Halaunbrenner (far left) and Mrs. Benguigui (second from left) inaugurate the Memorial to the Jews Deported from France at Roglit, Israel, on June 18, 1981.

Israel: June 18, 1981

On June 18, 1981, we inaugurated the Memorial to the Jews Deported from France, erected at Roglit, Israel, by the association Les Fils et Filles des Déportés Juifs de France (The Association of Sons and Daughters of the Jews Deported from France). On this moving monument, some 115 feet long and 13 feet high, are posted the names of the eighty thousand Jews who died as a result of the anti-Jewish persecutions in France. We insisted that the honor of unveiling the monument, whose facade was draped with an enormous cloth bearing the Star of David, go to two heroic and martyred mothers—Mrs. Benguigui and Mrs. Halaunbrenner.

Israel: February 5, 1983

By an extraordinary coincidence, it was at the memorial at Roglit that Mrs. Halaunbrenner, again in Israel, first heard, over her bus driver's radio, that Barbie had been returned to France.

Lyon: March 28, 1983

On March 28, 1983, the two mothers were with their attorneys in Lyon to register as associate plaintiffs against Barbie.

Opposite, below: Attorney Serge Klarsfeld, attorney Charles Libman, Mrs. Benguigui, Mrs. Halaunbrenner, attorney Richard Zelmati (hidden), and Alexandre Halaunbrenner, all participants in the struggle to bring Barbie to justice. Photograph by Progrès de Lyon.

Mrs. Halaunbrenner at the Memorial to the
Jews Deported from France, February 5, 1983.

MORE THAN FIFTY ADDITIONAL CHILDREN DELIVERED FOR DEPORTATION BY THE LYON GESTAPO IN THE FINAL MONTHS OF OCCUPATION

It occurred to me to study documents relevant to the Lyon Gestapo from the archives of the CGQJ (Commissariat-General for Jewish Affairs), which are now found in the Archives de France. The files of the CGQJ's Section for Investigation and Inspection, a veritable anti-Jewish police force, came in for particular scrutiny. In the files of the CGQJ's Lyon regional office, I found correspondence between the Lyon bureau of the UGIF and social welfare and refugee aid organizations, as well as with a number of police stations in Lyon.

From this correspondence I was able to draw up a list of Jewish children whose parents had been interned and whom the Gestapo's Lyon office was planning to transfer to Drancy for deportation. While awaiting this transfer, the Gestapo had no desire to burden itself with the children; instead of holding them at Fort Montluc, it remanded them into the custody of the UGIF. A UGIF social worker would then place them with a French family, or, more often, at the Hôpital de l'Antiquaille.

Then, when the Gestapo wanted to transfer the children to Drancy—with or without their parents—it ordered them picked up and brought back. Because the UGIF asked certain non-Jewish organizations to supply provisions for the trip, or because it had registered the children with the police stations in the precincts where they were placed, the children's names, as well as the dates of arrival for those who were brought to the Hôpital de l'Antiquaille, could be located.

The children are listed opposite, according to the month in which their names appeared in the correspondence. In parentheses is the number of the convoy in which they were deported, when that information could be ascertained.

March 1944:

PERLOFF, Claude-Gisèle
15 months (70)

VIVRAN, Sylvaine
5 months (70)

April 28, 1944:

*In question are five children who were to
leave Lyon-Perrache "next Monday morning,"
but whose names are not recorded.*

May 1944:

BENADON, Jean-Claude
5 months (75)

GAYERO, Régine
10 years (75)

GAYERO, Jacqueline
2 years (75)

LEVY, Marie
2 years (75)

VALID, Odette
13 years (76)

TOUITOU, Isidore-Isaac
13 years (76)

TOUITOU, Chaïm
13 years (76)

TOUITOU, Jeannot
12 years (76)

TOUITOU, Simon
10 years (76)

TOUITOU, Fernand
8 years (76)

TOUITOU, Josette
7 years (76)

TOUITOU, Louis
5 years (76)

TOUITOU, Gilbert
4 years (76)

KOPPEL, Margot
13 years (76)

LYON, René-Simon
2 years (76)

GOLDEN, Claude
4 years (76)

GOLDEN, Monique
12 years (76)

SAPOVAL, Jacques
6 years (76)

WOLFF, Pierre
7 years (76)

June 1944:

SHIPPER, Jacques
9 years (77)

BENSOUSSAN, Janine
3 years

ELLENBOGEN, André
9 years

The CHRIQUI children
ages unknown

BERNHEIM, Philippe
age unknown

July 1944:

HANDZEL, Marcel
9 years (77)

CAMHI, Victor
9 years (77)

SOWA, Adolphe
8 years (77)

HALIMI, Claude
11 years (77)

HALIMI, Jacques
9 years (77)

HALIMI, Josiane
6 years (77)

SANDMANN, Eddie
5 years (77)

CHEMLA, Robert
14 years (77)

CHEMLA, Huguette
13 years (77)

CHEMLA, Gilbert
10 years (77)

CHEMLA, Georgette
4 years (77)

SARFATI, Dario
18 months (77)

BENAYOUN, Jacques
13 years (78)

BENAYOUN, Marie
9 years (78)

BENAYOUN, Anne
5 years (78)

BENAYOUN, Lucien
2 years (78)

ABERGEL, Simon
9 years (78)

ABERGEL, Georges
8 years (78)

ZAJTMAN, Charles
10 years (78)

ALTHAUS, Guy
15 months (78?)

ALEXANDRE, Claude
19 months (78)

LAST, Cécile
8 years (78?)

FRABERGER, Claude
5 years (78)

HAYOUN, Gilbert
14 years

HAYOUN, Robert
10 years

HAYOUN, Jam
7 years

HAYOUN, Jim
4 years

BENSOUSSAN, Georges
15 years

BENSOUSSAN, Juliette
2 years

BENSOUSSAN, Emile
5 years

BENSOUSSAN, Georgette
8 years

BENSOUSSAN, Marie
9 years

ADDITIONAL TRANSLATIONS

Page 106, top:

Nice 200 5/16/44 245 = SA =

To the commandants of the camp for Jews in Drancy via the B.d.S. Paris.
Re: Jewess Odette Rosenstock born 8/24/1914 in Paris, last address in Nice 6 rue Gounot.
Previous: None.

The Jewess Rosenstock was with the transport which left here for Drancy on 5/2/44. As material could be collected in the meantime regarding her activities for a Jewish organization that was broken up in the south of France, I request that after transmission of the investigation report Rosenstock be interrogated in regard to the particular points and that a copy of the notes of the interrogation be transmitted here. The message will arrive in the coming days.

signed Dr. Keil SS Hauptsturmführer

Page 106, bottom:

SD - Marseilles No. 2634 4/4/44 7:15 P.M. - SR =

To the B.d.S. - IV B. - Paris. =
Re: Sommer, Andre, born 11/6/00 in St. Denis.
Last address in Marseilles, 56 Blvd. Notre Dame.
Previous: Telex No. 27,619 of 3/30/44 from B.d.S. - IV B there

The above was arrested on 3/11/4 in Marseilles as a disguised Jew. He was in possession of two I.D. cards, to one of which the stamp "Jew" had been applied in accordance with regulations. However, S. lived in a mixed marriage. He is a full Jew and will be sent to the Drancy camp for Jews on 4/1/44.

SD - Marseilles - The Commanding Officer
by order signed signature
SS Hauptscharführer

Page 107, top:

Security Police (SD)   *Lyon, 2/11/1943*
Lyon Office

To the
Commander of the Sipo-SD in the jurisdiction of the Military Commander in France—Paris
Re: Seizure of the Jewish committee "General Union of French Jews" (UGIF) Lyon.
Previous: None.
Encl.: 86 Arrest and Incarceration Certificates
80 Envelopes with identity papers and valuables and one inventory (in duplicate)

This office learned that there was a Jewish committee located in Lyon at 12 Rue Saint Catherine that supported emigrants and assisted Jews who wanted to flee from France into Switzerland in the preparation of their illegal border crossing. On 2/9/43 the seizure of this committee was carried out. At the beginning of the raid there were already over 30 Jews in the offices. Everyone was immediately taken into custody. In the course of another hour still more Jews appeared, and all together 86 people could be arrested. All those arrested were placed together in a room, and, before the personal searches could be undertaken, most of the Jews had destroyed their false identity cards and personal documents. Most of these Jews were intending to flee from here to Switzerland in the near future. During the search of the offices a greater quantity of valuables, foreign currency, and so forth was found; their owners are unknown. A part of the owners may already have fled into Switzerland. These valuables were confiscated and are enclosed in a separate envelope (see attached inventory). During the search of the individuals additional valuables and currency were found, which are enclosed in individual envelopes, together with the identity papers, for your further use.

All 86 arrested will be brought today to the military detention center at Chalon-sur-Saône and handed over.

As far as we were able to determine, the committee was supported by Jews in good financial circumstances in France and, above all, by a Jewish committee in Geneva.

As the military detention center in Chalon-sur-Saône is filled beyond capacity, the prisoners will, in accordance with a consultation with Chalon-sur-Saône, be sent on to the appropriate camp.

The leader of the Einsatzkommando
in the name (signed) Barbie SS Obersturmführer

Page 107, bottom left:

Lyon Urgent Telex No. 598 2/11/43 12:45 P.M. = Petr. =

To the B.d.S. Paris To the attention of SS Standartenführer Dr. Knochen. -
Re: Committee for the support of emigrants and destitute Jews
Previous: Telex order 7209 of Feb. 10, 1943, from there

As the move against the above committee was carried out by this office, the Jews were of course taken into German custody. —

The matter involves 86 people, who today will be transferred via Chalon-sur-Saône to the appropriate camp. —

The leader of the Einsatzkommando Lyon in the name signed Barbie SS Obersturmführer

Page 107, bottom right:

Security Police (SD)   Lyon, 2/15/43
Einsatzkommando Lyon

Log No. 563/43

To the
Commander of the Sipo-SD
in the jurisdiction of the Military Commander in France
Paris
Re: Seizure of the Jewish committee "General Union of French Jews" (UGIF) Lyon.
Previous: Memo from here of 2/11/1943 - Log No. 563/43
Encl.: None.

The arrest of 86 Jews was reported in our memo of 2/11/43. As the prison at our disposal, Montluc, was filled beyond capacity, the Jews were lodged in two rooms at Fort Lamothe. During the removal of the Jews to the railroad station, it was established that only 84 were still present. We were able to determine that in the early morning of 2/11/43, as they were being led to the latrines, two Jews escaped. Fort Lamothe is under the supervision of the Wehrmacht.

The escaped Jews are
1) Luxenburg, Aron, born 1/19/1893 in Lodz and
2) Driller, Siegfried, born 9/16/1896 in Vienna.

The investigations we have undertaken have not yet led to the rearrest of the two Jews.

Among the envelopes of currency and valuables which have been sent there are also those of the fugitives.

Please take note of the above.

The Leader of the Einsatzkommando: in the name (signed) Barbie SS Obersturmführer

Page 110, top:

Lyon 2743 4/15 12:28 A.M. - WE -

To the B.d.S. - Paris - IV B -
Re: Lodging of 1,000 Jews in Megève (Haute Savoie)
Previous: Telexed order No. 28061 of 5/12/43 from there - IV B - SA 225 LA

According to a communique from the delegate of the French authority for Jewish affairs in Lyon, the Italian authorities in Megève have up to now lodged in hotels 400 Jews, of whom 399 are of foreign nationality, for the most part German. The Jews were brought by bus from the Mediterranean coast (Nice, Cannes, etc.) to Megève. They are being supervised to the extent that a roll call takes place twice a day and a nine o'clock curfew has been set. Another 1,200 Jews are reportedly going to be brought to Megève from the Mediterranean coast. Negotiations in this regard are currently taking place between the French authorities and the hotel owners in Megève, because a proposal has been made to the Italian authorities on the part of the French to bring children from the French coastal cities, which are in danger of aerial attack, to Megève. Among the Jews are 12 who have long been sought by the French police. Nevertheless, the Italian authorities refuse to hand over these Jews.

Sipo-SD Einsatzkommando Lyon 1994/43 -
The commanding officer in the name signed Barbie, SS Obersturmführer

Page 110, bottom left:

Log No. 4232/43 - IV B - We/Bou.

To the
Commander of the Sipo-SD
in the jurisdiction of the Military Commander in France - Dept. IV B - Paris
Re: Jewish leaflet
Previous: Memo from here of 7/29/43 - Log No. 4232 - IV B - Encl.: 1 leaflet

The enclosed Jewish leaflet was delivered to this bureau today by the Commissariat-General for Jewish Affairs in Lyon.

in the name
(signed) Barbie

Page 110, bottom right:

Log No. 9305/43 - IVB - Ba.

To the
Commander of the Sipo-SD
in the jurisdiction of the Military Commander in France
in Paris
Re: Jews of Rumanian nationality
Previous: Telexed ordinance of the B.d.S. Paris, No. 78,299 of 12[?]/23/1943
Encl.: 1 memo from the Rumanian consul general in Lyon of Dec. 3, 1943

With reference to the ordinance cited above, I present a memo from the Rumanian consul general in Lyon, in which he communicates that orders have been given regarding Rumanian Jews who wished to return to Rumania and inquires whether this office had knowledge of same.

As nothing is known here in this regard, I bring this to your attention and await further instructions.

by order
(signed) Barbie
SS Obersturmführer

ABOUT THE AUTHOR

Serge and Beate Klarsfeld. Photograph copyright Jacques Zelter

Serge Klarsfeld was born in Bucharest, Rumania, in 1935. He spent the war years in France and was sheltered for a time in a Jewish children's home under the direction of OSE. He, his mother, and his sister survived the Nazi persecutions; his father, arrested in Nice in September 1943, was deported to Auschwitz, where he was murdered.

Klarsfeld studied history at the Sorbonne. He received the diploma of the Institute of Political Science in Paris; he also holds a law degree from the Paris Faculty of Law.

With his wife, Beate, a non-Jewish German, Serge Klarsfeld has campaigned throughout the world to bring Nazi criminals to justice. He is the author of *Vichy–Auschwitz*, an exhaustive study of the Final Solution in France, and of *Memorial to the Jews Deported from France, 1942–1944*, which lists the names and vital statistics of the 75,721 Jews shipped from France for extermination in Eastern Europe. Under the auspices of the Beate Klarsfeld Foundation (515 Madison Avenue, New York, NY 10022), he has published other detailed works on the Holocaust as well.*

In 1984, both Serge and Beate Klarsfeld were named to France's Legion of Honor. They were awarded the prestigious prize of the Foundation for French Judaism in the same year. Serge Klarsfeld is the president of the Association of Sons and Daughters of the Jews Deported from France.

The Klarsfelds live in Paris, where Serge maintains a law practice. They have two children: Arno, 20, and Lida, 12.

Included in the documentary record assembled by the Klarsfelds are the following publications: Kurt-Georg Kiesinger—Dokumentation über die P.G. no. 2 633 390 (Kurt-Georg Kiesinger—documentation on party member no. 2,633,390). 1969; Die Endlösung der Judenfrage in Frankreich—136 Deutsche Dokumente (The Final Solution to the Jewish Question in France—136 German documents). 1977; Le Mémorial de la Déportation des Juifs de France. 1978. (U.S. edition: Memorial to the Jews Deported from France, 1942–1944. 1983); The Holocaust and the Neo-Nazi Mythomania. 1978; Le Livre des Otages (The book of hostages). 1979; Die Endlösung der Judenfrage in Belgien (The Final Solution to the Jewish Question in Belgium). 1980; Vichy-Auschwitz—Le Rôle de Vichy dans la Solution Finale de la Question Juive en France (Vichy-Auschwitz—The role of Vichy in the Final Solution to the Jewish Question in France). Fayard, Paris, 1983. All publications by The Beate Klarsfeld Foundation unless otherwise noted.